Jesus's
TOUCH
of
INSPIRATIONS

PHYLLIS ANN WARD

WESTBOW
PRESS®
A DIVISION OF THOMAS NELSON
& ZONDERVAN

WestBow Press books may be ordered through booksellers or by contacting:

WestBow Press
A Division of Thomas Nelson & Zondervan
1663 Liberty Drive
Bloomington, IN 47403
www.westbowpress.com
844-714-3454

Scriptures taken from the Holy Bible, New International Version®, NIV®.
Copyright © 1973, 1978, 1984, 2011 by Biblica, Inc.™ Used by permission
of Zondervan. All rights reserved worldwide. www.zondervan.com The
"NIV" and "New International Version" are trademarks registered in
the United States Patent and Trademark Office by Biblica, Inc.®

ISBN: 978-1-6642-2235-9 (sc)
ISBN: 978-1-6642-2234-2 (e)

Library of Congress Control Number: 2021902134

Print information available on the last page.

WestBow Press rev. date: 02/12/2021

"Because he loves me" says the
Lord, "I will receive him.
I will protect him, for he
Acknowledges my name."

Psalm 91:14 (NIV)

Dedicated to Loved Ones in Heaven

Dedicated to God, Jesus, Holy Ghost, three in one,
Who helped me to write my Christian poems.
In loving memory of my mother,
Mildred "Millie" White.
She inspired me to write my Christian poems.
Love to my sister, Vickie,
My two nephews, Timothy, Phillip.
They always enjoyed my Christian poems.
Thanks to my nephew Phillip for his hard work
In helping me to get my poems put together.
Love to my sponsor daughter Leolyn
From the Philippines; she wants to be able
to read my Christian poems.
To all my loved ones in heaven,
The cover of this poetry book is about my mother's rainbow.
Why it's special to me is
It was on Memorial Day, and it had rained all day.
My mother had passed away at the hospital.
When we went home, it had stopped raining.
Our pastor pointed to the rainbow and said
To our family, relatives, friends, and I that "Jesus has
Received Millie into heaven this day."
Mildred "Millie" Robertson White
Born: March 26, 1929
Died: May 26, 2014, Memorial Day
Eighty-five years old.

The cover of this book represents
The rainbow goes up into the clouds
To show us that we can be received
Into heaven like Jesus had received
My mother into heaven.

A Father Who Cares a Lot

A father who cares more than just a little but a lot.
A father who will work all day.
A father who cares a lot.
A father who will do for me without
Complaints or want.
A father who cares a lot.
A father who loves and prays for
Me no matter what.
A father who cares a lot.
A father who goes to church
And praises the Lord.
A father who cares more than
Just a little but a lot.

An Old Year Has Gone, and a New Year Has Come

An old year has gone, and a new year has come.
Lord, help me through this new year just like you did the old.
Time goes by so fast.
With you, Lord, by my side, I know I'll
make it through this new year.
An old year has gone, and a new year has come.
Throw out the old year. I've had bad times. I've had sadness,
Trials, and tears.
Lord, you were there to help me through these times.
Throw out the old year; I've had happy
times, fun times, and laughter.
Lord, you were there all the time.
Lord, with you I've made it through the
old year, and you gave me peace
And joy in my heart, and I know it'll be the same this new year.
An old year has gone, and a new year has come.
When the old has gone, I've seen all you have done for me, Lord.
I want to always thank you and express my love for you
As each year that comes and goes.
You've always showed me your love, time
and time again, year after year.
An old year has gone, and a new year has come.
Lord, I don't know what will be in my life this coming year.
But I do know you'll always be with me.
An old year has gone, and a new year has come.
And just like the old year, so will it be the new year.

I'll have bad times, sadness, trials, and tears, and
I know you'll help me through them.
And just like the old year, so will it be the new year.
I'll have good times, happy times, fun times,
and laughter; you'll be there all the time.
And I'll still praise you and love you no matter what.

An old year has gone, and a new year has come.
As each year comes and goes, there is only one thing I know—
That I want to always serve you. I have you in my heart.
I love you and praise your holy name.
For I do know you love me, and you'll
be with me as the years go by.
Times goes by so fast.
An old year has gone, and a new year has come.
Until one of these years I'll live with the
Lord for all eternity in heaven.
And I'll praise your holy name.
An old year has gone, and a new year has come.

A Summer Get Well

It's summer outside.
I pray you'll get well
Real soon and that Jesus
Will give you sunshine
In your heart, summer
In your life,
And warm you with
His love, so I will
Send you a summer
Get well.

All Alone

All alone we can be, just you and me, Lord.
We can talk; I can sing for you to be praised.
All alone we can do many things, Lord—
Together, all alone, just you and me.
Where no one is but you and me, Lord.
All alone just to praise you, that's what it'll be.
All alone so I can pray to you, and
We can talk together.
To read my Bible, to read about you.
All alone in my mind, in my heart, out loud,
All alone, Lord.
I'll be with just you and me.
All alone, Lord, just you and me—that's
What it'll be.
All alone.

All Alone but Jesus

Even though I'm alone here on earth and only
My family wants me,
I have my Jesus and my Lord.
When I get to heaven, I'll never be alone.
I'll have my Jesus and my Lord.
Here on earth no one seems to want to be with me,
No one seems to care,
Only my family and my Jesus and my Lord.
When I get to heaven everything will change;
Everyone will want me and welcome me to my heavenly home.
I'll have my Jesus and my Lord.
What keeps me going here on earth is that I know that no one
Wanted my Jesus and my Lord.
What can I ask besides to be like my Jesus
And my Lord?
He went through more than me.
Then I can make it with Jesus by my side.
All alone but Jesus.

As You See Me, Lord

Help me to see myself as you see me, Lord.
Then, Lord, I will pray that I'll be better than I am.
Let people see you in me; I'll be what you want me to be.
Lord, help me live and serve you the way I should.
Lord, help me to pray and read my Bible so I will be like you.
Help me see myself as you see me, Lord.
Then, Lord, I will pray that I'll be better than I am,
To live close to you.
Help me see myself as you see me, Lord.

Baby Boy

Little is he, all cuddly and sweet,
Just for you to love and keep.
Bundle of joy he will always be.
He came from heaven above to make
Your home complete.

Baby Girl

Little is she, all cuddly and sweet.
Just for you to love and keep.
Bundle of joy she will always be.
She came from heaven above to make
Your home complete.

Baby Jesus

Baby Jesus's mother could of rode in a
Carriage with fringe on top with six white horses.
But she rode on a donkey.
Baby Jesus could have been born in a mansion.
But he was born in a stable.
Baby Jesus could have slept in a bed.
But he slept in a manger.
Baby Jesus could have worn royal clothes,
A purple robe, and a golden crown.
Baby Jesus could have been taken care of by a nanny.
Been born to a royal family.
But he wasn't; he was taken care of by his father and mother.
His father was a carpenter.
Jesus's earthly father, Joseph, taught him to be a carpenter.
Jesus lived a simple life.
Jesus is the King of Kings.
Jesus became a man, and he died on an
old rugged cross for our sins.
Then he rose up, and one of these days he will come back for me.
Jesus lives in heaven with his heavenly
father, God, and the Holy Spirit.
One of these days I'll live with Jesus in heaven for all eternity.
I'll wear a crown.
I'll live in my own mansion.
I'll walk on golden streets.
I'll praise my God, Holy Spirit, and Jesus.
Baby Jesus.

Because My Name
Is Written Down

My name is written down.
I was lost in sin.
But Jesus found me and saved me,
And brought me in.
Then my name was written down.
I was troubled and lonely, but Jesus found
Me and brought me in.
Then my name was written down.
Now I'm happy and free and saved by grace
Because my name was written down.
I'm bound for glory land to live for all eternity
With my Lord.
Because my name was written down,
When I get to the pearly gates, I'll meet my Jesus.
He will tell me to come on in to heaven's glory land.
Because my name was written down.
I'll walk on streets of gold and live in a mansion built for me
And wear a golden crown
Because my name was written down.
I'll sing with the heavenly choir.
I'll be with the angels and even my guardian angel
Because my name was written down.
I'll live with my loved ones and friends; I'll make new friends.
I'll live with all the Bible people
Because my name was written down.
I'll always praise and live with my Lord, Jesus Christ,
My heavenly Father, and the Holy Ghost for all eternity in heaven
Because my name was written down.

Bells That Ring

Bells that ring in time and space ring for all eternity.
Ring the good news—Jesus is coming again soon.
It may be soon, maybe just a little wait; it may be
A long time from now.
Bells ring loud, ring strong, and tell the good news
Of Jesus coming again.
Little bells, big bells, bells of many kinds
And sizes, ring loud and long, and tell the joyful news.
Jesus is coming soon for you and me.
Bells ring the joyful news of Jesus's coming.
Bells that ring.

Bible

Bible, you give me such joy and peace.
Bible, you have many things in you from
Chapter to chapter, verse to verse,
Cover to cover.
You have joy, sorrow, tears, laughter,
Sadness, happiness, peace.
Bible, you have many things for me to read.
When I'm down, when I'm up, through tears, through laughter,
Bible, you help me through all these times.
Dear Bible, thank you for each person, each thing
You have written in you.
For these things help me through all times.
Bible, you know just how I feel about what's in you.
Bible, you give great joy to me; you tell me the
Most important things of all about my Lord,
Jesus Christ, and how God gave his Son to die
On the cross for my sins.
Thank you, heavenly Father, for my Bible.

Bubbly, Bubbly

Bubbly, bubbly inside of me, Lord.
That's the way I feel; I can't explain,
But you understand.
Bubbly, bubbly inside of me, as though
I want to cry and laugh at the same time
Inside and outside.
Bubbly, bubbly, I want to smile and jump
And run with joy.
I feel I have special secrets inside of me.
I want to share my joy with others.
I just can't explain how I feel the joy, peace,
Love, when I feel bubbly, bubbly
Inside and outside.
With my laughter and crying I feel bubbly. Bubbly.
I never want to lose the way the Lord helps me
Express how I feel.
Bubbly, bubbly inside and outside, the happiness,
The joy, the peace.
The love and thankfulness I have for the Lord.
Bubbly, bubbly, I don't want to stop feeling
The bubbly, bubbly inside because that's how
I want how I want to always
Praise the Lord.
Bubbly, bubbly.

Candle of Light

Candle with flames of light, show forth your life.
Show your light to a lost and lonely world.
Make your light bright; let them see in
The darkest of night.
Candle, let them know you care that they're in a
Lost and lonely world.
Candle, show your light of love; let them know
You'll bring them in.
The lost and lonely people of the world
Look to the candle of light, follow the light
Of God.
Candle of light will lead you to the God of love.
Candle, show forth your light
To the lost and lonely world.
Candle of light.

Candle So Bright

Candle with fire of light, show your light at night so bright.
At day of light.
Show forth your flame; don't die out, bring forth your
Light so bright.
Saved ones like the candle show forth the flame of
Light; don't die out.
Let God be your light; show forth your love,
Your salvation, concerns, cares, and prayers.
Saved ones be like the candle with fire of light.
Show your light at night, so bright at day of light.
Bring in more candles, and let them shine.
Bring in the lost; saved ones, let them shine for God too.
Candle, shine your light so bright.

Children So Free

Children, you will always be so free.
In the sunlight, cool blowing breeze,
You will feel God's close to you wherever you are.
Little children, you will be so free
To come and be of God's children, that he will love you so.
Little children, run, laugh, be so free as you should be.
One of God's children to love.
So full and free as you should always be one
Of God's children, you will always be.
Children so free.

Christian Flag

Christian flag stand tall, stand true, blow in the wind;
Stand for Christian liberty.
I, as a Christian, stand true, blow in the wind
For you, heavenly Father, to spread the Word.
Christian flag stand true to the heavenly Father.
Lord, help me to stand true to you too.
Help me stand for truth and liberty.
Christian flag, stand for truth and liberty.
Christian flag, stand true to our heavenly Father.
Help me stand true to the heavenly Father.
Christian flag.

Christmas Gift

Christmas does not mean receiving gifts or giving gifts.
Even though it's nice to do.
But the most important thing of all is having
Christmas together with you.
That's what Christmas is all about to me,
Loving each other, caring about each other.
Christmas is being here for each other.
This Christmas gift is for you, my family.
Even more important of all about Christmas is
That Jesus was born a babe in a lonely manger for us.
And that Jesus is in our homes and lives.
That's what Christmas is all about.
So, dear Jesus and my family, have a very Merry Christmas.
This is my gift to you.

Citizenship in Heaven

Citizenship in heaven—that's what I have, that's where I'm going.
My citizenship is beyond the sun, moon, stars, and sky.
My citizenship is where I cannot see yet.
My citizenship is in heaven; it's the most beautiful
Place of all.
My Jesus is in heaven; that's where my citizenship will be.
I'll be there with my Jesus.
I'm not of this world; I have a citizenship in heaven
With my Jesus.
Citizenship in heaven—that's what I have, where I'm going.
Praise Jesus's holy name; He died on the cross and rose for me.
He forgave me of my sins.
Praise his holy name, he gave me citizenship to heaven.
In the end,
Citizenship in heaven—that's what I have, that's where I'm going.
I have citizenship in heaven.

Come Follow Us

Come follow us.
We've got some good news to tell.
Jesus is risen; he's our Savior.
He saved us from our sins.
Come follow us.
We've got some good news to tell.
He can make you happy within.
Go to church, learn about his Word.
Pray to him, read the Bible.
Be happy within; get right with God.
Come follow us.
We've got some good news to tell.
You'll be in heaven with him.
Come follow us.
We've got some good news to tell.
Come follow us.

Come with Me, Jesus

Come with me, Jesus.
Take my hand, and walk with me
As we talk.
Along the sunny beach by the ocean,
We feel the sand through our toes as
We look for seashells by the seashore.
We feel the breeze on our faces.
As we walk along the way, we watch
The sun goes down and the sun come up.
Such peace as Jesus and I walk
Along the beach.
Come with me, Jesus; take my hand,
And walk with me as we talk.
In the deep forest we see
And hear wild animals all around us.
We hear the wind whistling through
The trees.
As we walk along the way we watch
The sun go down and the sun come up.
Such peace as Jesus and I walk through
The forest.
Come with me, Jesus; take my hand and
Walk with me as we talk upon the mountaintop.
We can see as far as the eye can see,
Mountain after mountain.
I'll yell on the mountaintop, and you'll hear the echoes
Of my praises to you, Jesus, as we stand on the
Mountaintop.
As we stand on the mountain, we watch the sun go down
Behind the mountains and the sun come up from

The mountains.
Such peace as Jesus and I walk on the mountain.
Come with me, Jesus; take my hand and walk with me as we talk.
As we walk through the desert, we feel the hot sand under our feet.
We see dust balls going past as we go through the dust storm.
We feel the dry hot wind and the hot sun on our faces.
As we walk along the way, we watch the sun
go down and the sun come up.
Such peace as Jesus and I walk through the desert.
Come with me, Jesus, and take my hand
and walk with me as we talk
Through the prairie, where the wildflowers and green grass grow
And sway in the wind.
As we walk along the way we watch the sun go down and the
Sun come up.
Such peace I feel with you by my side.
Come with me, Jesus; take my hand and walk with me
Everywhere I go.
I tell you I love you and feel the peace and love you give me
As we walk along.

Come with me, Jesus; take my hand and walk with me
Through my life because life is like a beach by the ocean.
I feel calm.
But sometimes the ocean is rough, and I feel unsafe.
But sometimes the ocean is smooth, and I do feel safe.
Life is like being in the forest; I feel so afraid.
Life is like a mountain; I feel really happy.
Life is like being in the desert; I feel all alone.
Life is like being on the prairie; I feel at peace.
Jesus will give me peace during all these times

Of my life.
Come with me, Jesus; take my hand and walk with me
As the pearly gates open wide as we walk
Into heaven.
Come with me, Jesus; take my hand and walk with me.
Talk with me on the street of gold by the crystal sea.
Come with me, Jesus.

Coming of Jesus

Coming of Jesus.
Star of Jesus shining bright.
Born on that long-ago Christmas night.
As shepherds look up in the sky, what do they
See? A star brighter than all.
The angels come singing and praising the Lord.
Hallelujah to the King of Kings.
The three wise men bring Jesus gold, frankincense,
And myrrh, and give him glory and praise
As Mary and Joseph stand by Jesus in his manger.
As Jesus slept peacefully, the angels sing to Jesus
Praises of his coming to earth.

Don't Close the Little Country Church Doors

Don't close the church doors on the little country church.
Someone pleaded, "Pray and trust in the Lord.
Someone please brings in the lost sheep.
Don't close the doors on the little country church.
Will someone please get on their knees and pray
For the lost sheep to come home, trust, and obey the Lord.
Let him call you to bring in the lost sheep.
Ring the little country church bell; call all the lost sheep in.
Don't close the little country church door."
Someone kneeled and prayed, "Bring in the sheep.
Let them know the Lord.
Don't close the little country church doors."

Don't Doubt

Don't doubt, don't doubt; bury it in the deepest sea.
Don't bring them out anymore.
Jesus will see you through.
Don't doubt, don't doubt; bury it under a rock
On the mountainside.
Don't bring them out anymore.
Jesus will see you through.
Don't doubt, don't doubt; bury it under the lava of a volcano.
Don't bring them out anymore.
Jesus will see you through.
Don't doubt, don't doubt; bury it in a blizzard storm.
Don't bring them out anymore; Jesus will see you through.
Don't doubt, don't doubt; bury it in an ice storm.
Don't doubt, don't doubt; bury it in the rainstorm.
Don't bring them out anymore; Jesus will see you through.
Don't doubt, don't doubt.
Jesus will see you through.

Ears to Hear

He who has ears to hear, let them hear
The sound upon their ears, the trumps
Of his coming.
To eternity of heaven for the ones who
Have ears of his coming again.
O the joy that will be when he comes again
For us.
O the ears to hear of Jesus's coming,
O the joyful notice that will be.
Ears that can hear listen for his coming
again for those who live for him.
See him: There, did you hear him coming again?
Well listen really close for he's coming again.
What joy that will be.
Ears to hear he's coming again.
Ears to hear.

Easter in My Soul

Easter is over with for one more year, or is it?
Easter is in my soul every year
For all earthly years.
Easter every year will come and go.
But never gone from my soul; it'll always be
Easter in my soul.
My Lord will rise in my soul and heart
Every second, every minute, every hour,
Every month, every year, for all eternity.
Easter in my soul is for always; it will never go from my soul.
Easter is over with for one more year, or is it?
No, Easter is never over; it is within my soul for always.
The Lord raises up in my life and in my soul for always.
Easter is over for one more year, or is it?
No, Easter is always in my soul for always.
Easter in my soul.

Easter Morn

Easter morn, when they went to Jesus's grave,
Expecting to see him, they came to pay their respects.
But what did they see on that Easter morn?
All that they saw was an empty tomb
And the linen cloth.
Why was that, how could that be? they wondered.
How afraid and confused, where was their friend Jesus?
This Easter morn, some saw an angel,
Can you believe telling them, "Don't be afraid"?
"Jesus, your friend you're looking for is not here.
But he has risen, like he said he would."
One saw Jesus but thought he was the gardener.
One Easter morn she asked, "Where did you lay him?"
He said to her on this Easter morn, "It is I, the One you
seek, Jesus, your friend."
Praise Jesus's holy name.
He rose from the grave to set us free from our sins.
Praise him; he will come again to take his children
To heaven to live for all eternity.
So let's praise Jesus's holy name this Easter morn.

Flag of America

Flag of America, you stand for liberty and justice.
Flag of America, stand for freedom and love.
God gave America our flag to serve him and
Freely go to church, read our Bibles, pray,
And tell others about him.
Flag of red, white, and blue, stand true.
Thank you, God, for the flag of America,
It stands for freedom of choice to serve you.
Flag of America.

For Me

Thank you, Jesus, for dying on the old
rugged cross for my sins
And rising victorious for me,
A sinner to be saved.
For me you shed your blood, and your
Body was broken; oh, the pain you must
Have gone through.
The nails went through your hands and feet.
The spear in your side; Jesus, you did it all for me.
Jesus, how can I ever tell and show you
My thanks for dying this way for me,
For you hanging there all alone on the old rugged cross?
Now Jesus, that cross is the most beautiful cross
Because you hung there for me, Jesus.
You rose from the dead.
For me, Jesus, you're alive for me.
For me, Jesus, you'll come back to take me
To heaven to live for all eternity.
I want to praise you, Jesus.
For me.

For You

I love you because of you.
I care for you because of you.
Jesus, whisper to me, "I'm here for you.
I died on the cross and shed my blood for you.
Then I rose for you, I live for you on this Easter morn.
I forgive you of all your sins.
I'm always here for you.
I'm glad you let me come into your heart.
I'll come for you and take you to heaven
With me for all eternity.
I do it all for you.
For you."

For All He Did

I can feel the teardrops falling down my face
As my Savior took my place.
He forgave me instead of crucifying me for my sins.
I knew then he cared for me, no matter what I did.
I'm a sinner saved by grace.
He was crucified on an old rugged cross for our sins.
Instead of sending me,
I put him there because of my sins; he said,
"Forgive them, they know not what they did."
He will take me home to heaven one of these days
So I can see him face-to-face to thank him
For all he did.
One of these days I want to kiss his nail-printed feet
So I can tell him I love him because he first loved me.
For all he did.

Give Him Glory

Give him glory! Give him glory!
Give him praises upon high.
My Lord deserves more praises than I know how to give.
Give him glory! give him glory!
Praise his holy name.
Sing his praises, sing hallelujah to the King and
Savior Jesus Christ.
I want to give thanks for all things.
Praise his holy name.
Give him glory! Give him glory!

Glory, Glory, Hallelujah

Glory, glory, hallelujah, the gates of heaven
Open wide for me to enter in.
Glory, glory, hallelujah, heavenward I go.
Lord, help me to be ready for your coming again.
Help me to live and be what you want me to be.
Glory, glory, hallelujah, the gates of heaven
Will be opened wide for me to enter in.
Lord, help me to wait and pray.
Help me to tell others about you
so they can enter heaven's gates too.
O to see the gates of heaven open wide,
To live in heaven to praise the Lord,
In heaven for all eternity.
Glory, glory, hallelujah, the gates of heaven
Open wide for me to enter in.
Glory, glory, hallelujah.

God Made Them All

God made you and me to feel our love for him
And his love for us.
He made the bees to make the honey to eat.
He made the trees and leaves to shade us from the sun.
He made the sun to warm the earth.
God made them all.
He made the sky so blue, the clouds so soft and white.
The rain to keep the earth fresh.
The rainbow for a promise.
God made them all.
He made the stars to shine at night, the moon so bright.
The grass so green.
The flowers so beautiful and smell so pretty.
The birds to fly and sing his praises.
All the animals of the world, wild or tame,
There for us all to enjoy.
God made them all.
The fish to swim in the lakes, streams, and oceans.
God made them all for us.
God gave us air to breathe, eyes to see,
Ears to hear, and a nose to smell.
God gave us family, relatives, and friends to enjoy.
God made them all for us to love.
God gave us ourselves.
God gave us all his only Son, Jesus.
God made them all for us to enjoy.
God made them all.

God Made So Many Things

God made the sun and the moon, the stars in the sky.
God made so many things for us.
God made the flowers, bees; he made the grass and the leaves.
God made the nuts and the trees.
He made so many things for us.
God made the animals and the insects.
God made the fields and the prairies.
God made the corn, wheat, beans, tomatoes—
So many more things to eat.
God made so many things for our use.
God made the water and oceans, streams, and waterfalls.
God made the land and mountains.
God made so many things for us.
God made you and me for all these things.
He gave us breath of life.
God made so many things.

God Made You Special, Lillian

God made you special, Lillian.
God made you special with your bright smile
And sunshine face.
God made you special with your kindness and thoughtfulness.
God made you special, Lillian.
God made you special with your words of comfort and advice.
God made you special with your teaching and preaching.
God made you special, Lillian.
God made you special with your concerns for others.
God made you special because of your
friendship and love for others.
God made you special, Lillian.
God made you special because you make others feel special.
God made you special for the special things you do.
God made you special, Lillian.
God made you special because you tell others about him.
God made you special because others can see him in you.
God made you special, Lillian.
God made you special because you let him live in your heart.
God made you special because of your sweet
spirit and your close walk with him.
God made you, that's why you're special.
God made you special, Lillian.

Dedicated to a lady from my church named Sister Lillian.

Good Morning, Lord

Good morning, Lord, it's a new day to praise you.
A new day to pray, read my Bible.
Good morning, Lord, thank you for keeping me during the night
For I know you'll keep me during this day.
Good morning, Lord, it's a new morning to tell others about you.
God morning, Lord, it's a new day to love
you more, and you to love me.
Good morning, Lord, it's a brand-new day to live for you and draw
Closer to you.
Good morning, Lord, it's a new day to feel you in my heart.
Just to thank you for being there for me.
Good morning, Lord, it's a brand-new day to praise you.

Heavenly Things

Walk through the pearly gates.
Walk the golden streets.
Play on the golden piano; sing in the holy choir
With a voice so sweet.
Talk with the angels so pure.
Play with all the animals.
Talk with all the Bible people and with all
The saints above.
Talk with loved ones.
Mostly talk with Jesus.
Kneel and kiss Jesus's feet, thanking him for everything.
The joy of being in heaven for all eternity.
Giving praises to the Lord and Savior,
Will be happiness beyond words.
Heavenly is more than words can tell.
Heavenly things.

Hear Ye! Hear Ye!

Hear ye! Hear ye!
Hear all about it! I've got good news to tell.
Your sins can be forgiven; you can go to heaven.
Jesus came to earth as a babe,
Then died on the old rugged tree.
Then he rose and went to heaven.
He will come again for you and me.
Hear ye! Hear ye!
Hear all about it; I've got good news to tell.
There's a Savior who loves you and me.
I've a Savior who can live in your heart
And give you peace and joy.
There's a Savior who cares.
Hear ye! Hear ye!
Hear all about it. I've got good news to tell.
Jesus lives for you and me.
Your sins can be forgiven.
Jesus will be back to take us to heaven.
Hear ye! Hear ye!
Hear all about it; I've got good news to tell.
Jesus loves you and me.
Hear ye! Hear ye!

Help Me Be a Plant

Plant of green leaves is healthy.
Lord, help me to be a healthy plant!
Help me to grow and flourish.
Lord, help me not to be a plant that dries up
And turns yellow, then brown, then leaves drop
Off one by one.
Lord, that's the way some Christians are when
They don't pray to you or read your Word,
The Holy Bible, or go to church.
Then they go back on the Lord; they stop growing.
But then, Lord, when there are leaves that need
To be picked off, when there are things that are wrong
In my life, Lord, you take care of it and help me drop
Off the leaves in my life that don't belong there.
Lord, help Christians to be a healthy plant, keep
Growing, having more leaves, grow greener, taller,
And bigger; Lord, that's the way Christians are when
They pray, read your Bible, go to church.
Lord, help me be a healthy and a flourishing plant
To grow for you.
Help me to be a plant.

How Do I Know He's the Lord?

How do I know he's the Lord?
I know because he lives within my heart.
He gives me peace and joy within.
How do I know he's the Lord?
I know because he takes away my fears.
He mends my broken heart.
How do I know he's the Lord?
I know because he lifts my burdens.
He heals my sickness and pain.
He answers my prayers the way he sees
Best for me.
How do I know he's the Lord?
He does so many wonderful things.
How do I know he's the Lord?
I know because he saved me
And sanctified me from my sins.
How do I know he's the Lord?
I know because he came and lived
On earth as a man.
He shed his blood on an old
rugged cross, and died and
Arose again for me.
How do I know he's the Lord?
One of these days he will come again for me.

Then I'll live for all eternity in heaven.
How do I know he's the Lord?
He loves me so.
The Bible tells me so.
This is how I know he's the Lord.

Hummingbird

Hummingbird, humming its praises, its flowers.
Hummingbird always on the go, telling others about the flowers.
People can be like the hummingbird, humming
Their praises to the Lord.
People can be like the hummingbird, be on the go,
Telling others about the Lord.
Hummingbird flying from one flower to another flower.
People can go from one person to another person, telling
Them about Jesus.
People singing their praises to the Lord.
Hummingbird, humming its praises.
People can be like the hummingbird
And give their praises to the Lord.

Hurry! Hurry!

Hurry! Hurry!
All around God let me just pause for a while
For a word of prayer, to feel you by my side.
Hurry! Hurry!
That's what some days seem, but with you
By my side, I don't have to worry.
Hurry! Hurry!
Away I go, some more; let me stop and pause
For a word with you, God; let me feel you by my side.
Hurry! Hurry!
But can't get anywhere, God, let me stop and pray
With you by my side.
Hurry! Hurry!
God, let me pray with you by my side.
Hurry! Hurry!
Once again, I praise your name, God, you're by my side.
Hurry! Hurry!

I Can't Comprehend

All the pain you must have gone through,
I can't comprehend.
You loved me so much to give your life.
And you said, "Forgive them, they do not
Know what they do."
I can't comprehend.
Even though I was not there that day,
I'm still to blame.
He still loves me so, to die in my place.
The nails, the spear, the thorn crown—
The pain of it all.
I can't comprehend.
Praise the Lord.
Hallelujah he rose. "He is not here,"
The angel says, "He's alive, praise
His holy name."
He arose for me.
I can't comprehend.
He loves me so; he's alive,
He arose, hallelujah, praise
Jesus's holy mame.
I can't comprehend.

I Don't Know Why

So many troubles and hurts and don't why.
Only I'm glad that God is on my side.
The trials, and when things go wrong,
You don't know where to go or what to do.
Only you pray to the Lord to help you through.
Let him show you what to do.
You don't know why this has to happen.
But you know the Lord, know he's there
to see you and me through.
Lord, I don't know why, and I shouldn't ask.
But I know you will make me strong in you.
With my physical hurts, Lord, you were there to help and protect.
I know you'll always work things out for the best.
I don't know why; Lord, just help me to
stand true and be strong in you.
I don't know why, but it'll all be worth it when I get to heaven.

I Feel Your Hand in My Hand, Jesus

I feel your hand in my hand, Jesus.
I can feel the nail prints on your hand.
I know it's because you died and arose
for my sins, and I'm forgiven.
I feel your hand in my hand, Jesus.
Then I take your hand to let you know
That I'm glad that you understand.
I feel your hand in my hand, Jesus,
When I cry or feel sad and all alone.
And when I'm scared and afraid,
And confused.
I know you understand.
I feel your hand in my hand, Jesus.
When a loved one or a friend has gone
On before me.
When a loved one, a friend, or I'm sick.
I know you understand, Jesus.
I feel your hand in my hand, Jesus.
When I'm happy, when I have a good time
And have fun, or when I laugh.
I know you understand, Jesus.
I feel your hand in my hand, Jesus.

When I pray to you, when I read my Bible.
When I go to church and listen to your Word.
When I teach little ones about your love for them.

I know you understand, Jesus.
I feel your hand in my hand, Jesus.
When I tell others about you, and when I pray for their souls.
When I have old Christian friends and new Christian friends,
And I pray for them.

I Feel Your Hand in My Hand, Jesus

I know you understand, Jesus.
I feel your hand in my hand, Jesus.
How do I know you understand?
I know because I feel the nail prints on your hand,
And I know you gave your life for me; it was when you
Gave me your hand, Jesus.
I feel your hand in my hand, Jesus.

I Just Want You to Know

"I just want you to know that I love you so.
That's why I come, to let you know that
I care for you too.
Now you'll know that I died on the old rugged tree.
That's why I love you so.
Then I rose for you to show I really care for you.
I just want you to know that I love you so.
I'm your Savior and Lord."

"Thank you, Jesus, for letting me know
That you care for me, and thank you, Jesus,
For loving me so.
Thank you, Jesus, for letting me know."

I Knew My Name
Was Called

I knew my name was called by my Father above.
I heard a quiet voice, whispering my name.
If I listen real close, I'll hear his voice of comfort and love.
I knew my name was called from my Father above.
I'm glad to hear his quiet voice calling my name
And helping me each day, his words of wisdom,
His voice of cheer.
I knew my name was called from my Father above,
Asking me to live for him and serve him well,
Asking me to help others to hear his quiet voice
And live for him.
I knew my name was called from my Father above.
I knew my name was called.

I Know My God
Is With Me

I know my God is with me.
Down in the valley I know that's
Not where I want to be, but I still
Know my God will be with me.
Up on the mountain, that's where
I'd rather be; I know my God is with me.
He sees me through the good times.
He sees me through the bad times.
I know he loves me wherever I might be.
When I feel all alone, that I'm not loved,
But praise my God, I really do know
That my God is with me, and he love me.
I know he cares for me; he looks after me.
I know my God is with me.
He sees my tears and feels my fears.
He tells me he will wipe away my tears
And take away my fears.
For he's with me through everything.
He tells me, "Don't worry, my child, I love you.
I'll always be with you, no matter what
Comes your way."
I sometimes think, *What am I going to do?*
I don't know which way to go.
God tells me, I'm here with you. I'll show you
Just in time what to do, that I'm taking care of you.
Just relax in my loving arms.

I will take care of you."
I know my God is with me.
He tells me, "Have faith and believe I will take
Care of everything.
I will make you strong in me."

I Know My God
Is With Me

He will always see me through my ups and my downs.
I will have faith in you, my God, for I know you
Will be with me through every part of my life.
I praise God's holy name for always being with me.

I know God is with me.
*I sometimes think, What am I to do? I don't know
Which way to go.*
I pray, "Please help me, God. Show me what to do."
God tells me, "I'm here with you.
I'll show you just in time what to do.
I'm taking care of you."

I Love You, God

I love you, God.
I love you God because you first loved me.
I love your kindness, your caring.
I love you, God.
I love you God for you gave your Son.
I love God for let your Son die on the cross for my sins.
I love you, God.
I love you, God, for your goodness.
I love you, God, for you forgave me all my sins.
I love you, God, for now I'm yours, and you're mine.
I love you, God.

I Miss You, Mom

I miss you, Mom.
I feel all alone.
I feel so sad without you, Mom.
I miss your hugs, your love.
I miss your prayers, our talks.
I miss you, Mom.
Thank you, Mom, for teaching me about Jesus.
I miss your smile, your laughter.
I miss our time together, the fun we had.
I miss everything about you.
In my heart you'll always love me, pray for me.
I'll always love you, Mom.
I miss you, Mom.
Thank you, God, for giving me the mom that you gave me.
Mom, I wouldn't want any other mom than you.
You're the best mom in the world.
You were my best friend.
Thank you, God, that I'll see my mom again in heaven.
One of these days, for all eternity.
I miss you, Mom.

I Want To

I want to praise your holy name,
Give your name, praises above all names.
I want to bow down before you, and kiss
Your nail-print feet.
I want to sing your praises in the holy choir.
I want to walk the golden streets as I talk with you.
I want to play with your holy animals.
I want to talk with the people who are in your Holy Bible.
I want to talk with my loved ones and friends.
I want to do so many wonderful things in the heavenly kingdom.
I want to say thank you for everything.
I want to praise your holy name.

I Was There All the Time

"I felt all alone and that no one cared.
But you were there all the time, Jesus."
"Yes, I was there all the time."
"My tears would fall; my heart was breaking.
I was sad all the time.
You were there all the time, Jesus."
"Yes, I was there all the time."
"I felt I couldn't go on with life.
I didn't know how much more I could take.
You were there all the time, Jesus."
"Yes, I was there all the time."
"I felt you had left me, Jesus.
But you were there all the time, Jesus."
"Yes, I was there all the time."
"Then I didn't know where else to turn.
You were there all the time, Jesus."
"Yes, I was there all the time.
I had my arms around you.
You just need to lean on me.
I was telling you that I care for you
And that I love you.
And I'll always be there for you. I'll
Never leave you, and I'll always love you.
I was there all the time."
"You were there all the time, Jesus."
"Yes, I was there all the time."

If You Had Not

Thank you, Jesus, for coming to earth as a babe
In a lonely manger, wrapped in swaddling clothes.
If you had not done this, where would I be?
Leaving your heavenly Father, telling others
About God's love.
Healing the sick, forgiving the sinners, making
Them your own.
Thank you, Jesus, for dying on the old rugged tree.
Rising again in three days, you walked the earth for a while.
Thank you, Jesus, for I know you will come back for me.
If you had not done this, where would I be?
Now I can tell
Others about you.
They can live for you.
Thank you, Jesus, for I can live for you.
If you had not done this, where would I be?
Thank you, Jesus, for loving me, saving me, sanctifying me.
Thank you, Jesus, for forgiving me of my sins.
If you had not done this, where would I be?
So I say thank you so much, very much, for loving me that much.
You will come for me; I'll live in heaven with you for all eternity.
Thank you for doing this for me.
If you had not done this, where would I be?
If you had not …

I'll Be Home Real Soon

The road might be rough and rocky.
Life might not be smooth or easy.
But I'll be home real soon.
Life is not an easy road to live.
Your burdens of life you have to go through,
But Jesus is there to help you through.
I'll be home real soon.
You'll have the mountaintops and then the valley.
The road of life is winding and steep.
But Jesus is there to help me through.
I'll be home real soon to be with Jesus.
I'll be home real soon.
Jesus will take my hand and say, "Welcome
Home, my children."
I'll be home real soon.

I'll Be There Too

When you go that way, I'll be there too.
Toward heaven's gates, I'll meet you there.
If you get there before me, meet me there.
Tell my loved ones and friends I'll be there too.
I'll sing praises to Jesus, my Savior.
I'll sing with the heavenly angels in their
Heavenly choir.
I'll walk the golden streets.
If I get there before you, I'll meet you there.
If you get to heaven before I do, meet me there.
Tell my loved ones I'll be there too.

I'll Meet My Jesus

As I ride on the great speckled bird,
I'll come to the pearly gate so pure.
I'll meet my Jesus with robe made of white.
A crown made of pure gold.
My name will be written on the pages of God's Word.
My Jesus will meet me at the pearly gate
And we'll walk the streets made of pure gold.
We'll talk of the great things he has done.
He'll tell me of a mansion he's built for me.
My Jesus, I'll bow down at your nail-print feet.
I'll kiss your nail-print feet.
I'll tell you thank you for giving me a mansion
In heaven and a crown made of pure gold
And walked with me on the streets of gold.

I'll Never Let Go, Jesus

I'll never let go, Jesus.
When the trials come, the pressures of life come,
I know you'll be there for me.
I'll never let go, Jesus.
When there's pain, hurting,
I know you'll be there for me.
I know you'll ease the pain and hurt.
I'll never let go, Jesus.
When there's sadness and sorrow,
And the tears don't seem to stop,
I know you'll give me peace
And joy again.
I'll never let go, Jesus.
Sometimes I feel like giving up
And wondering, *What's the use?*
But I keep on going and keep on
Trusting and believing, knowing that Jesus
Is there all the time to help me through
Everything in my life.
I'll never let go, Jesus, because I know
You'll never let me go.
I'll never let go, Jesus.
No matter what happens,
I'll never let go, Jesus.
Thank you, Jesus, I feel
You are hanging on to me.
I feel your loving arms around me.
I'll never let go, Jesus.

I'm a Little Bit Closer Today Than Yesterday

I'm a little bit closer today than yesterday.
I feel closer to Jesus's love for me.
I'm closer to feeling more of his loving arms
Around me to make me feel safe.
I'm a little bit closer today than yesterday.
I feel closer to his kindness and goodness to me.
I feel joy in my soul; I feel his peace of understanding
In my heart.
I'm a little bit closer today than yesterday.
I'm closer to trusting him more and more.
I'm closer to believing him more and more
That he will always take care of me,
My loved ones, and friends no matter
What comes my way or theirs.
I'm a little bit closer today than yesterday.
I'm closer to Jesus by serving him when
I read my Bible and pray to Jesus more and more.
I'm closer to him when I go to church
and teach Sunday school class.
I'm closer to him when I sing his praises.
I'm closer today than yesterday.
I'm closer to Jesus when I tell others about him
And pray for them and pray for their souls.
I'm a little bit closer today than yesterday.

I'm a Little Donkey

I'm a little donkey.
Who am I that Jesus would choose me
To ride on? I feel so blessed.
I'm a little donkey.
The excitement and the joy I felt
Carrying Jesus through Jerusalem.
I saw many people waving their palm branches
And laying their robes down
As they praised him.
I'm a little donkey.
Even though it wasn't for me—it is all for Jesus—
It made me still feel happy.
It was Jesus being praised.
It made me feel special that I was part of it all.
I'm a little donkey.
I know that Jesus loves everyone,
And I know that he loves me too.
Hearing people praise Jesus,
And I praise him, too,
During Palm Sunday.
I'm a little donkey.
I know I'll be with Jesus in heaven
One of these days.
As I walk the golden streets,
I hope he will let me carry him through heaven.
As I hear all the angels and the saints praise Jesus,
I will praise Jesus too.
I'm a little donkey.

I'm a Little Drummer Boy

I'm a little drummer boy, and poor am I.
I have nothing to give to baby Jesus.
All I can do is play my drum for thee.
Pa-rum-pum-pum.
I'm a little drummer boy.
I'm not worthy to come to thee.
The three wise men can give their
Gold, frankincense, and myrrh.
They're so much more worthy
To come before thee.
I'm a little drummer boy; all
I can do is play my best for baby Jesus.
So all I can do is play my drum for thee.
Pa-rum-pum-pum.
The shepherds are so much more worthy
To come before thee.
I'm a little drummer boy; all I can do is play
My best for baby Jesus.
Pa-rum-pum-pum.
Even the donkey that carried Mary
Is more worthy to come before thee.
I'm a little drummer boy; all I can do
Is play my best for baby Jesus.
Pa-rum-pum-pum.
Even the cow and sheep are more worthy
To come before thee.
I'm a little drummer boy; all I can do is play
My best for baby Jesus.
The angels who sang your coming and the angels
In heaven are more worthy to come before thee.

I'm a little drummer boy; all I can do is play
My best for baby Jesus.
Pa-rum-pum-pum.
Mary and Joseph, I'm a little drummer boy.
Poor am I.
I have nothing to give, so all I can do is play my best
For baby Jesus.
Pa-rum-pum-pum.

I'm a Little Drummer Boy

I praise thee, God, for giving baby Jesus; you
Know I'm a little drummer boy, and poor am I.
All I can do is play my best for baby Jesus.
Pa-rum-pum-pum.
Everyone else can give their finest gifts to thee.
Baby Jesus, I'm a little drummer boy, and poor am I.
All I can do is play my best for baby Jesus.
Pa-rum-pum-pum.
Pa-rum-pum-pum.
Pa-rum-pum-pum.

I'm Going to Heaven, and You Can't Stop Me

I'm going to heaven; you can't stop me.
Jesus lives in my heart and life, so I'll serve
Him, and you can't stop me.
I'm going to heaven, and you can't stop me;
No, you can't stop me.
My God, my heavenly Father, my Lord and Savior
Jesus Christ, my Holy Spirit, three in one want me
To live in heaven for all eternity with them.
No, you can't stop me; no, you can't stop me.
Angels will take me to heaven one of these days,
And you can't stop me; no, you can't stop me.
I'll walk through the pearly gates one of these days,
And you can't stop me; no, you can't stop me.
I'm going to heaven, and you can't stop me.
No, you can't stop me.
My Jesus will meet me in heaven when I first
Get there one of these days.
I'll kiss Jesus's nail-pierced feet when I
First get to heaven.
And you can't stop me; no, you can't stop me.
I'm going to heaven, and you can't stop me,
No, you can't stop me.
I'll wear a white robe and a golden crown in heaven
One of these days; you can't stop me, no you can't stop me.
I'll live in a mansion that God has built for me one of these days.
I'm going to heaven, and you can't stop me; no, you can't stop me.
I'll walk upon those golden streets one of these days.

I'll see the crystal-blue sea and the mountains so rugged
One of these days.
I'm going to heaven, and you can't stop me; no you can't stop me.
I'll live with my loved ones and old friends and new friends
One of these days.

I'll live with all the angels in heaven and thank and live with
My Guardian one of these days.
I'll sing in the heavenly choir.
I'll praise God, Jesus, and the Holy Spirit.
I'm going to live in heaven for all eternity one of these days.
My prayers are that I'll meet you in heaven one of these days.
I'm going to heaven, and you can't stop me; no, you can't stop me.

I'm Home at Last

I'm home at last.
Home at last, that's where I'm now.
The pearly gates are open wide as Jesus is waiting
For me with some of my loved ones.
I'm home at last.
I can see Jesus's smiling face, his arms open wide.
I'll kiss his nail-print feet.
"Come on in, my child, for you're home at last
To walk the golden streets."
He will have a mansion built for me.
What I see, words I cannot tell.
O the glory of being home at last.
No more tears, no more fears.
No more tears or burdens to bear.
I'm home at last.
I'll sing of joys unspeakable.
The joy of being with God my Father,
Jesus my Lord and Savior, the Holy Spirit.
The joy of being with loved ones and friends.
I'm home at last.
The joy of being with the holy angels
And my guardian angels.
I know it'll be hard, but don't cry for me,
My loved ones.
I've prayed that one of these days you'll
Live with me in heaven for all eternity.
Thank you, Jesus, for bringing me home
At last.
I'm home at last.
Home at last.

I'm Home at Last

I'm home at last.
The pearly gates are open wide
As Jesus is waiting for me with some of my loved ones.
I'm home at last.
I can see Jesus's smiling face, his arms open wide.
"Come on in, my child, for you're home at last
To walk the golden streets."
He has a mansion built for me.
What I see words I cannot tell.
O the glory of being home at last.
No more tears, no more fears,
No more trials or burdens to bear.
I'm home at last.
I know it'll be hard, but don't cry for me, my loved ones.
I've prayed that one of these days you'll live with me
In heaven for all eternity.
Thank you, Jesus, for bringing me home at last.
Praise your holy name, Jesus.
I'm home at last in heaven.
I'm home at last.

I'm Living for Him

I'm living for him on the banks of the Jordan.
I'm living for him on the shores of Galilee.
I'm living for him wherever I live.
I'm living for him on the mountaintops.
I'm living for him in the valley.
I'm living for him whatever life might bring to me.
I'm living for him wherever he may lead me.
I'm living for him for he died for me.
I'm living for him for he rose victorious from the grave.
I'm living for him, so I can praise him forever.
I'm living for him because he's coming
back for me one of these days.
I'm living for him for he lives within my heart.
I'm living for him because one of these days I'll live
In heaven with my family, relatives, and friends.
Even new friends in heaven for all eternity.
I'm living for my Jesus because he's my friend, Lord, and Savior.
I'm living for him.

Impression on Me

I look up as you sit in the church pew.
I love to see you sometimes raising your arms, saying,
"Hallelujah," or jumping up, saying, "Praise the Lord."
I love to see you clapping your hands together and saying, "Amen."
Sometimes you just sit, quietly trusting the Lord.
Or nodding yes.
O how wonderful it is to see you sitting there in the church pew
As you sing for the Lord or pray to the
Lord, trusting him, or praying
With others, waiting for God's answers.
I love to hear your testimonies of what God has done.
O what a wonderful Christian you are.
I'll always remember you.
I look up front as you sit in the church pew.
You make a good impression on me.

About an older lady who went to the same church as I did.

In a Twinkling of an Eye

In a twinkling of an eye, the trumpet will sound.
Jesus will come from the East;
He will come for his loved ones.
In a twinkling of an eye, Jesus will take us
To heaven through the pearly gates for all eternity.
We will walk the streets of gold
In a twinkling of an eye.
Each of us will have a mansion built for us.
We'll wear a golden crown.
In a twinkling of an eye,
We can sing in the heavenly choir.
I'll talk with my guardian angel
In a twinkling of an eye.
I'll be with my family, relatives, friends,
And I'll make new friends
In a twinkling of an eye.
With God, the Holy Spirit, and Jesus,
I'll praise them for all eternity.
In a twinkling of an eye.

Jesus Is Just on Time

Jesus is just on time.
Jesus is never too early;
He's never too late.
Jesus is just on time.
It doesn't matter what happens in our lives,
If we go through good times, if we go through bad times.
Jesus is never too early, he's never too late.
Jesus is just on time.
Just like Noah when he built the ark.
The rain came pouring down and flooded the earth.
God made a promise with a rainbow.
Just like Shadrach, Meshach, and Abednego, who Jesus
Protected from the fiery furnace.
Jesus is never too early; Jesus is never too late.
Jesus is just on time.
If we pray and trust Jesus,
He will answer our prayers the way he sees best for us.
If we even have faith as a mustard seed,
Jesus will see us through no matter what.
Jesus is never too early.
Jesus is never too late.
Jesus is just on time.
Just like Moses leading his people through the desert
To the Promised Land.
Just like Joseph in the pit and when he was in prison,
And living in Egypt, the famine.
Jesus is never too early, he's never too late.
Jesus is just on time.
Jesus was never too early or too late; he was always
On time during Bible times.

Jesus was never too early or too late; he was always on time
With people before us.
Jesus will never be too early or too late; he will always be on time
With people during my time.
Jesus will never be too early or too late; he will always be on time
With people after my time.
Jesus will never be too early or too late; he will always be on
Time with all Christian people.

It may seem the answers to our prayers may not come on time.
It's not too early, but it's too late; it's not on time.
We think some things should be a certain way, which
Is our way, when Jesus sees it another way.
Then we see that Jesus's way is far better than our way.
We might think it should be now, not later, but Jesus knows
It's better for us to be later.
Jesus is never too late.
He's never too early.
Jesus is just on time.
Jesus, I want to praise your holy name for answered prayers
And for doing what is best for us.
Jesus, I want to praise your holy name for never being too early
And never being too late, but just being on time.
Jesus is never too early; Jesus is never too late.
Jesus is just on time.

Jesus Is My Engineer

My life is like a train on a mountain railroad
When the train curves around the mountainside.
My life is like I'm on a train on a mountain.
There's lots of curves in my life.
Jesus is my engineer.
Life is like a train on a mountain railroad,
When the train climbs the steep mountain.
That's when I'm on the top, and my life is on top and happy.
Then the train goes down the steep mountain, and it's
In the valley.
That's the way that my life is; I go down in the valley, and I'm sad.
Jesus is my engineer.
He runs my life, and he helps me through the bad and good times,
When I'm on the top of the mountain or down in the valley.
Life is like a train on a mountain railroad.
The train goes through dark tunnels.
My life is like I'm on a mountain railroad; I sometimes
Go through dark tunnels.
Life is like a mountain railroad.
When the train goes through the dark tunnel, it will come
To the sunlight out of the tunnel.
My life is like when I'm in the dark tunnel, and then
I come out of it into the sunlight.
Jesus is my engineer,
He helps me travel through life.
Life is like a train on a mountain railroad.
It goes through the narrow part of the mountain.
My life is the same way; I go through the narrow
Part of my life.
Jesus is my engineer.

Life is like a train on a mountain railroad.
The train goes smooth and straight through the mountain.
My life sometimes goes smooth and straight.
My life is like a train on a mountain railroad.
The train has a conductor to take care of you
While you're on the train.
In my life I have a conductor; my guardian angel
Is my conductor.
My guardian angels take care of me and keep me
Safe when I know it and when I don't know it
All through my life.
Life is like a mountain railroad.
Jesus is my engineer.

The engineer on the mountain railroad, see the train
Through the mountain.
Jesus is my engineer, and he sees my life
Through all my trials, and he gives me victory.
Jesus is my engineer.

Life is like a train on a mountain railroad.
The train makes stops and let's passengers off
And let's passengers on.
That's the way life is; a loved one or a friend passes away.
When a person gets saved, they get on the train of life with Jesus.
Life is a mountain railroad.
The train goes homeward bound.
That's how life is; we're homeward bound to heaven.
Life is like a mountain railroad.
The train comes to the station and makes the final stop.
People gets off and go through the gate so
they can go where they want to go.
Jesus is my engineer.
He stops at the train station. I'll get off the train of life.

I'll go through the pearly gates into heaven,
to my new home, to live for eternity.
I'll be with all my family and friends.
I'll praise and thank Jesus, my engineer, for
bringing me through my railroad of life
And for bringing me to my heavenly home for eternity.
Jesus is my engineer.

Jesus Is Our Gift to Us

When angels come and sing the joyful songs
On this Christmas morn,
The angels tell the joyful news of Jesus's birth.
Bright dreams abound as Jesus is born.
Jesus is our gift to us.
Peace surrounds as the angels announce Jesus's birth
In a manger long ago on Christmas morn.
Jesus is our gift to us.
The shepherds came this Christmas morn.
The three wise men gave gifts of gold, myrrh, and frankincense.
A bright star shines brightly over a lonely stable.
Joseph and Mary watch close by as Jesus
Sleeps in a manger this Christmas morn.
So this Christmas morn, let us give ourselves to Jesus
As a gift to him.
Jesus is our gift to us.

Jesus Knocking

Jesus knocking on my heart's door.
"Come in," I say, "come in to stay.
I won't make you wait.
I'll have you come right in to stay."
Jesus knocking on your heart's door.
Please don't you let him wait.
Have Jesus come in; let him give you peace
Like he did for me.
Jesus knocking on my heart's door.
Thank you, Jesus, for knocking on my heart's door
And coming in.
Jesus is knocking on your heart's door.
Jesus knocking.

Jesus, My Pilot

Jesus, you're the pilot of my life.
Guide my life the way it should be.
Let me go straight and true.
Jesus, my pilot, doesn't let me go back
Or to the left or right.
Guide me through the narrow and straight path.
Heaven-bound I must go.
Jesus, pilot of my life.
If I come to paths unknown, bring me back
To the straight and narrow.
Heavenward bound I must go to meet God, my captain,
To live and rest from the long life of stress.
Jesus, my pilot, leads me heaven-bound.
Jesus, my pilot and my friend, heaven-bound I will go.
Jesus, my pilot.

Jesus, Please Help Me

Jesus, please help me live as you
Want me to live.
To be what you want me to be.
Go where you want me to go.
Jesus, please help me always to praise
Your holy names as you want me to praise you.
Help me to give as you want me to give.
Jesus, help me to love you the way you want me to love you.
To love others as you want me to love others.
Jesus, please help me to honor you as you want
Me to honor you.
To bow down and praise you the way you want me to
Bow down and praise you.
Jesus, please help me to tell others about you
As you want me to tell others about you.
To teach Sunday school to little ones and tell
Them about you as you want me to teach Sunday school
To little ones and tell them about you.
Jesus, help me to go to church, read my Bible, pray, and
Sing your praise as you want me to go to church, read my Bible,
Pray, and sing your praises.
Jesus, help me to live so others can see you in me
As you want me to live so others can see you in me.
Jesus, please help me.

Jesus, Take My Hand

Jesus, take my hand; lead me to the path
That you want me to go.
Jesus, take my hand; don't let go.
Guide me through sorrow; make me strong.
Guide me through happiness; help me stand true.
Jesus, take my hand, lead me, guide me, never let me go.
Jesus, take my hand through hard times, through all the tears.
Through good times, through all the laughter.
Jesus, through all times, take my hand, and never let me go.
Jesus, take my hand.

Jesus Will See You Through

You never know what might be.
But Jesus will see you through
The good times, the bad times.
Whatever it might be, Jesus will
See you through.
You feel like laughing, you feel like crying.
You feel so down and blue.
You feel like jumping for joy and singing hallelujah.
Jesus will see you through.
Praise his holy name.
He will bring you through everything.
Just trust and lean on him.
Have some faith, and never doubt, never fear.
Jesus will see you through.

Jesus, You're Many Flowers

Jesus, you're a rose of Sharon to me.
You're the lily of the valley.
You're a violet that smells so sweet.
Jesus, you're a daisy that shines in the sun.
You're a silver bell that rings all year long.
You're a morning glory that shows the glory
Of your face.
You're a day flower that is with us all day long.
You're a closed gentian; you keep us safe
At the close of day and all night long.
You're a mountain laurel; you're always on the mountain,
Looking down, watching us, keeping us safe.
Jesus, you're different kinds of flowers
Because you made them all for us.
Jesus, you're many flowers.

Just a Whisper Away

Just a whisper away, call on Jesus.
When you're down and low,
When you're happy and free,
Jesus is just a whisper away.
Just call on Jesus.
Talk with him about everything and anything.
No matter what, he loves to talk with you.
Jesus is just a whisper away.
It makes you closer to him,
It makes you feel like friends
When you talk with him.
He's just a whisper away,
Just call on Jesus.
He's the Almighty; he's the King of Kings.
It doesn't matter, he listens to you.
Call on Jesus, he's a whisper away.
We should be still and listen.
Let him talk to you; it will be worth it all.
Let him whisper to you.
He has lots of things to say worth listening to.
He's just a whisper away; just call on Jesus.
Just a whisper away.

Just Imagine

Just imagine if you were there.
The anguish the Christian people
And his disciples must have felt.
The Savior being crucified.
The waiting to see what would happen.
The anguish when they went to the tomb
And Jesus was gone.
Then, oh! The angels said, "Jesus is gone.
He is not here.
He is risen!"
Praise his name, Jesus is alive.
Just imagine how they felt—
The happiness, the joy, the confusion.
Just imagine how they felt.
Glory hallelujah, Jesus is alive!

Key to Happiness

Who holds the key to my happiness?
Jesus holds the key to my happiness!
When I'm sad, Jesus makes me happy.
When I cry, he helps me to laugh.
Who holds the key to my happiness?
Jesus holds the key to my happiness.
When burdens seem too heavy,
He lifts them off my heart.
When there seems to be many trials,
Jesus helps me through them and bears me up to them.
Who holds the key to my happiness?
Jesus holds the key to my happiness!

Key to Heaven

Jesus has the key to heaven for me and others
To enter in, by my witness, my life to show for others to see.
The key to heaven I want to share with others.
Jesus has the key for him to open heaven's pearly gate
For others to enter in, and for me to enter in.
The key to heaven Jesus has for us; follow
me, and we'll follow Jesus
With the key to heaven.
The key to heaven is what I share with
others about how to get saved,
And you ask Jesus into your heart.
With the key to heaven, Jesus opens heaven's
pearly gates for us to enter in,
To be with him for eternity.
Key to heaven.

Kite of Life

Kite flying high, right up to the sky.
Kite flying free, that's the way my
Soul shall be.
With the Lord in my soul, I feel free
As a kite in the sky.
Kite with the string attached, guide me.
You will not wonder afar; you'll
Stay straight on course.
Lord, that's the way I want to be.
I want to be like the kite, and you
Have the string to my life.
Lord, you keep me on the
Straight course of life for you.
Kite fly high, right up to the sky,
With you, Lord, guiding me.
Lord, I'll be like the kite.
You guide my life.
Kite of life.

Lead Me, God

Lead me, God, my feet the way they should go.
My hands to love, my arms to hug.
Lead me, God, my eyes to see what's only right.
Lead me, God, my mouth to say only things
That are kind; let me smile for you.
Lead me, God, my ears to ears to hear only what's kind and good.
Lead me, God, my heart for kindness and love for you and others.
Lead me, God, only the way you want me to be.
Lead me, God, myself, my all, my everything, and my life.
Lead me, God.

Let Go, Let Me Work

"Let go, let me work."
"Never stop, never ends, how much more is there?
Is it ever going to get better?"
"Let go, let me work, my child."
"I don't know how much more I can take!
Sometimes I feel all alone; I feel sad, I cry.
Oh, why do I feel like this?"
"Let go, let me work, my child."
"One thing or another seems to happen.
I don't know why.
When is it ever going to get better?"
God says, "Let go, let me work."
"I pray here, God, I'm tired, I'm weary, I'm worn.
Forgive me, God, I'm sorry; I'm tired of fighting
My own battles.
Help me to always let you work in my life."
"Let go, let me work, my child.
Rest in my arms, my child."
"Yes, God, I'm finally letting go and letting you work.
I'm all yours; do what you see is best for me.
Help me not to take it all back again."
"Let go, let me work."

One more time, even though I've said it
before, I want to say it again.
Thank you that I can live all eternity in heaven with my loved ones
And friends and angels.
Especially that I can live with you, my Lord
Jesus Christ, my heavenly Father God,
And Holy Spirit.
I want to say thank you for everything.
One more time, even though I've said it before,
I want to say it again. Thank you.

Liberty and Justice

Dear Lord, give me liberty and justice.
The freedom to pray to you.
The freedom to sing about you.
Dear Lord, you give me liberty and justice.
The freedom to go to church and serve you.
The freedom to tell others about you.
The joy of peace in my heart and soul.
The love I can have for others and to show others the way.
Dear Lord, you give me liberty and justice.

Life Is Stairsteps to Heaven

Life is stairsteps to heaven.
Each step up we take, the closer we get to heaven
When we ask Jesus into our hearts.
One step is easy to take as our lives seem easy to take.
Next step up is hard to take as our lives seem hard to take.
But we do step up because we know Jesus is with us.
We don't know what life will be like as we
Take each step up.
Jesus tells us, "I'm always with you," as
we take each step in our lives.
"I'll never leave you or forsake you."
Life is stairsteps to heaven.
Each step up we take we know Jesus will take with us.
The next step up our heart feels broken with sorrow and grief.
We feel alone on that step, but Jesus remains with us.
"I'm with you, my child, on this step of
your life; you're never alone."
The next step up we take we believe and have faith in Jesus
Because you know Jesus is with us on the stairsteps of life.
Life is like stairsteps to heaven.
The next step up there are sickness and pain.
You feel alone, but Jesus remains with us; you're never alone.
"I'm with you on this step of your life."

The next step we take we have happiness, peace, and joy.
We know Jesus is with us on this step of our lives.
When we cry or when we laugh, Jesus is with us on this step
Of our lives as we step up.
Jesus is always with us on each step we take, that
We do take on the stairsteps toward heaven.

Then we're on the last step of the stairs of our lives.
We're at the top.
Jesus is holding out his hand to take our hands to lead
Us through the pearly gates into heaven.
Jesus is telling us, "Welcome home, my child. It's worth each step
Up the stairs of life you took because you'll live in heaven for
Eternity with me."
Life is stairsteps to heaven.

Lighthouse

Lighthouse that shines its light at night,
Light searches for boats at night.
Searches for souls that are lost.
Just like when God searches for souls
That are lost from him.
Lighthouse that stands tall and light so bright,
Search for me out in the night.
So dark, the water so cold.
Thank you, God, for searching for me,
Finding me in the darkness of sin.
Now I can give a light so bright from my heart,
Just like light from the lighthouse.
Search for my soul in the night, so dark, water so cold.
Lighthouse that shines its light at night.
Lighthouse shine your light.
Search for souls for God.

Like an Eagle

Like an eagle as wings soar to the sky.
Just like our souls with our Lord in our hearts
Soars to the sky.
The eagle never looks back; we're it wants remained.
A sinner, when his soul has gained height,
When from his sin to the Savior has given, never looks back.
From sins and woes he looks on to new
Heights untold.
New depths, new goals for the Lord to heaven above.
The eagle soars from lofty heights to life untold.
Trusting our Lord, believing in him,
Doing what he knows is best for us.
Just like an eagle.

Little Angel on Christmas Day

Little angel has some good news.
There's a little baby born this Christmas morn.
He's Jesus Christ, our Savior.
He's here to save you from your sins.
The shepherds had already come to bow down to worship him.
The three wise men who come gave him
gold, myrrh, and frankincense.
See the other little angels, they're were
there to give him gifts of songs
Of praise of his coming on this Christmas Day.
See the bright star? It's up in the sky, overlooking
The town of Bethlehem.
There, do you see under the stars so bright?
You'll see a manger with baby Jesus in his mother Mary's arms.
Beside them there's Joseph, He's there to take care of them.
There are the sheep and cows; they seem
to know why baby Jesus is there.
There's the donkey that carried Mary;
he felt special for what he did.
So this Christmas Day, let's give ourselves to God
As a gift to him because Jesus is his gift to you.
Little angel and the other little angels
praise Jesus this Christmas Day, and you can praise
Jesus this Christmas Day.

Little Bell

There was a little bell that would not ring.
I asked her one time, "Why don't you ring?"
She said, "Maybe, maybe I could ring, but there's
Only one thing: I cannot ring."
I asked her then, "What is this one thing?"
She said to me, "I cannot ring because,
I have nothing to ring for. I have not what
Other bells have—the Savior, Jesus.
I do not know him, so that is why I cannot ring.
I don't have the joy other bells do."
"Well," I said to her, "let me tell you the story of
Jesus and how he was born a babe and then died
A man on a cross for souls to be saved.
Then you can ring, Little Bell, as other bells do."
I told her and she asked, "Is that all I have to do?"
I said, "Yes. Would you like to have him come in?
Then you can ring your bell of salvation for him."
She said yes, and you know what?
He came in, and Little Bell is now ringing her bell
Of salvation for her Savior, Jesus.
She told me, "Thank you for sharing with me.
Now I can share with other bells too.
I'll ring my bell for him so others can hear."
Ring, ring, ring!
The Christ will come again, for you and for me.
Ring, Little Bell.

Little Bird

Little bird, so soft and fine.
As I look in your cage,
You sit so quietly, knowing you're God's
Soft and sweet.
Knowing God made something so fine.
Your feathers so gray, brown, and white.
Little bird, flying around your cage.

Little Drops of Dew

Little drops of dew that are on the green,
Green grass, wet and cool.
Little drops of dew, like little diamonds
In the green grass.
Dear God, thank you for each little drop
Of dew, each different, each made in their
Own little ways.
Little drops of dew that stand on each
Blade of green grass,
How wet, how cool when I walk through
The green grass with drops of dew.
When I walk through the wet green grass,
I see how God made the little drops of dew
Look like rainbows in the green grass.
Like little diamonds in the green grass.
Little drops of dew.

Lord Be the Anchor of My Soul

Lord, be the anchor of my soul.
Drop the anchor deep in my soul.
Make it steadfast and sure,
Just like the anchor of the ship,
When it hits deep in the ocean bed,
It'll there to stay.
Anchor of my soul, my Lord,
You will be.
Put your anchor deep within my
Heart to stay.
Don't let go; keep it steadfast and sure.
Just as the anchor of the ship, Lord, be
The anchor of my soul.

Lord, Thank You

Lord, thank you for keeping me safe through this day
And each day.
With kindness you show me through the little things and
The big things.
You, Lord, keep me safe and help me through each day.
You're there through bad times and good times.
Lord, you're there with my ups and downs.
Lord, thank you for keeping me safe—
whatever comes, whatever goes.
You're there through the thick and the thin.
Keep me from all harm.
Lord, thank you for keeping me safe.
Lord, thank you.

Lord, Let Me See

Let me see others as you want me to see them.
Help me see only the good in others and not the bad.
Lord, help me to tell others about you
That they will know the way of salvation.
Help me not to think or feel bad about people.
Lord, let me see others as you want me to see them.
Help me to see only the best in others.
Even if they don't feel or see the best in me,
Lord, help me see the best in them.

Mend a Broken Heart

Mend my broken heart,
Lord, that is what you do.
My heart seems so heavy,
With trials to load me down.
Lord, you mend my broken heart
When things seem too much.
The pressures of life,
The trials, burdens, my heart
Seems to be broken in two.
Lord, mend my broken heart.
Make it right once again.
Lord, I give you my broken heart,
My all, whatever it might be.
Lord, mend my broken heart.
Thank you, Lord, for mending
My broken heart, for mending
It once again.
For mending it each time
I need it.
Thank you, Lord, for my
mended heart.
I know you'll always mend
My broken heart.
Mend my broken heart.

Mend My Broken Heart, Lord

Mend my broken heart, Lord.
My heart seems so heavy and loaded down
With sorrow and sadness.
Mend my broken heart, Lord.
When life seems too much and my heart
Seems to break in two, mend my broken
Heart, Lord.
Make my heart over anew.
The pressures of life, the trials and burdens,
I carry them all; it seems too much for me.
Help me to give them all to you.
Mend my broken heart, Lord.
I give you my broken heart, oh, Lord.
Give me peace and happiness in my
Heart once again.
Make my heart over anew.
Help me to trust you and feel you close to me.
Thank you, Lord, for mending my broken heart,
For making it over anew.
Thank you, Lord, for making it over anew.
Thank you, Lord, for always being there for me.
Thank you, Lord, for always loving me.
I love you, Lord.
Thank you for mending my broken heart, Lord.

Mirror of Reflections

Mirror that see reflections see the tiniest things.
Others can see the reflections of Christ, see the tiniest
Things of me.
I want to live my life for Christ, be like the mirror.
Mirror that sees me, show how I really am; Lord,
Help me to be like thee, see you in me.
Mirror that sees my reflection.
Christ, help me be like the mirror; let them see you through me.
Let me be a reflection for the Lord.
Mirror of reflection.

More Than Just a Mother

You're my mother, but you're more than just that.
You're my friend.
You're my mother, but you're more than just that.
You're the one I can talk to when I need too.
You're my mother, but you're more than just that.
You're the one who taught me about God.
And you're my mother, but you're more than just that.
You love me, and I love you.
You're my mother, but you're more than just that.
You're everything to me.
You're more than just a mother.
You're my friend.

Mother

You give a song in my heart and joy in my soul.
You're a mother of all mothers.
You give happiness to me.
Mother, I'm glad God gave me to you.
You cared enough to love me, to pray,
To worry, to care, to do little things,
Big things for me.
Mother, you're a mother of all mothers.
You're everything to me; I love you more than
Words can say or I can show.
Mother, I give you a mother's day, every day because you're
Special to me.
Mother, I'm glad you showed me the way of salvation.
I'm glad God gave you this gift of being the best mother
In the world.
You're a mother of all mothers to me.

Dedicated to my mother, Millie.

Mother Like Mine

No one would ever dream to have a mother like mine.
She's so loving, kind, sweet, and understanding.
When I need someone to understand me,
When I'm sad, she's there to brighten me up.
When I laugh, she laughs with me.
She's always there for me.
She understands; she cares for me.
She's sweet, kind.
She talks with me.
She has a wonderful smile.
She cheers me up.
Lord, thank you for a mother like mine.
Mother like mine.

Mother Like Mine

No one would ever dream to have a mother like mine.
She is so loving, kind, and sweet—also she is understanding.
When I need someone to understand me, or when
I'm sad, she's there to brighten me up.
And she is there to understand; she does just that.
Don't you wish you had a mother like mine?
To have someone to love you, and you love her.
To have someone to care for you.
A mother who just understands and is sweet and kind.
If you need a mother to talk to you, I'll let you talk to mine.
She'll listen and understand you too.
I'm glad I can have a mother like my mother,
With a smiling face to cheer me so.
Lord, thank you for a mother like mine.
Help me, Lord, to be a mother like my mother is to me.
Mother like mine.

Mustard Seed

Faith of a mustard seed, see what
It can do.
Pray to God and then trust in him.
Even if it's a faith of a mustard seed, many
Things it can be for you.
Your mustard seed of faith will grow
When times go on.
Bigger, bigger your mustard seed will become.
So will your faith in God grow.
As your faith in God will grow.
Faith in God as a mustard seed will grow.
Faith in God as a mustard seed will grow.
Mustard seed.

My Father

My father is kindness and fun.
He's everything a daughter would want.
My father is caring and loving.
He's just what I want for a father.
My father is tall and strong.
My father is noble and right.
He's just right for a father.
He's a thoughtful and praying father.
My father is everything a daughter would want.
Thank you, God, for my father, who's everything to me.
Thank you, heavenly Father for my earthly father.
My father.

My God Is Bigger

My God is bigger than the mountain, bigger than the oceans.
My God is bigger than the world, bigger than the universe.
My God is bigger than my problems; he's big enough to
Keep me safe from all harm.
He's big enough to take care of me.
My God is bigger than anything that comes my way.
He's big enough to see me through them all.
My God is big enough for me.
My God is bigger.

My Guardian Angel

Thank you, God, for giving me my guardian angel.
I can't thank you enough, my guardian angel, for always
Being here for me when I need it, and always protecting me.
Thank you, my guardian angel, for being there when I'm in
trouble or going to be hurt, and you protect me.
Thank you, my guardian angel for all the things in the past
That you were there for me and protecting me from harm.
Thank you, my guardian angel, for all things in the future
That you'll be there for me and you'll protect me.
Thank you, my guardian angel, for all the times from the past
That you protect me when I didn't know about it.
Thank you, my guardian angel for all the times in the future
That I will not know about when you'll protect me.
Thank you, my guardian angel for loving me that much,
For always being here for me.
I love you, my guardian angel, not only for always
Being there for me and protecting me,
But because you're my guardian angel and you're you.
You're very special to me.
Thank you, my guardian angel.

My Little Feet

My little feet.
God made my little feet.
My little feet will walk in the
Steps that Jesus walks.
My little feet.
My little feet can walk
With my family to church.
I can hear and learn more
About Jesus in church.
I can listen to my preacher
As he preaches the Word.
I can sing praises.
My little feet.
My little feet can walk
To Sunday school class.

My Sunday school teacher
Can teach me about Jesus's
Love for me.
My little feet.

My Little Hands

My little hands.
God made my little hands.
My little hands.
My little hands can fold as
I pray to Jesus.
My little hands.
My little hands fit into
My daddy's and mommy's
Bigger hands.
They make me feel safe.
My little hands.
My little hands hug
The ones I love.
My little hands.
My little hands can feel
Jesus's hands in my hands,
And I can feel his love for me.
My little hands.

My Mother

Memories of all the things you do and did for me.
Of your love you show to me.
The prayers you prayed on your knees for me.
Helping me when I need you.
Every concern and loving deeds.
Remembering you holding me, hugging me,
Caring for me; you'll always do this because
You love me.
Mother, you're many wonderful things.
There are so many things, there's no way
Of putting them all down.
But my mother is the most special
Mother in the world.
There are never enough words
To say how much I love you, Mother.
You taught me about Jesus
And his love for me.
Mother, you're my friend.
You're my mother, and
I love you.

My Mother's Eyes

When I see my mother's eyes,
I see them twinkle like stars
Of love she has for me.
Her eyes twinkle like stars of caring
Over the years, from before I was born
Until now, and even years to be.
Thank you, God, for the twinkle-like
stars of love in in her eyes.
Thank you, God, for her eyes of kindness
And caring.
Thank you, God, for her eyes that twinkle
Like stars.
Years long past, years to come,
Long years to be, I'll always see the twinkle
Like stars of love in my mother's eyes.

My Mother Is a Rose

My mother is a rose.
A rose's petal is soft to touch.
My mother's face is a petal.
My mother is a rose.
The fragrance of a rose is like how
sweet my mother seems to be
With her sweet smile.
My mother makes me warm and safe.
My mother is a rose.
The different colors of roses are like the different ways
my mother shows me she loves me.
My mother is a rose.
Mother, here's a rose for you.
That's what you made me.
Thank you, Mother, for making me a rose too.
My mother is a rose.
Thank you, God, for making my mom a rose.
Thank you for helping my mother help
Make me into a rose too.
My mother is a rose.

My Mother Told
Me about Jesus

My mother told me about Jesus.
When I was a baby, my mother held me in her arms.
Then she told me about Jesus and how Jesus loves me
For the Bible tells me so.
When I was a little girl, I sat on my mother's lap, and she
Told me about Jesus and how Jesus cares
for me; the Bible tells me so.
My mother prayed with me and for me.
My mother sang, "Jesus Loves Me."
I sat at my mother's knees as I listened to my mother as she told me
That Jesus loves me for the Bible tells me so.
My mother read me Bible stories as I listened to her.
My mother tells me that she loves me, that's why she tells me
About Jesus and that Jesus loves me, too,
For the Bible tells me so.
My mother told me about Jesus.

My Poems

Poems of many kinds—short, long,
Sad poems into happy poems.
That's what some of the poems
The Lord helps me write.
But most of all, my poems.
Are always about my Lord.
He's the One who really helps
Me with my poems.
The Lord just puts them in
My mind, and I start writing them.
When they come to me, I pray, and the
Lord helps me write them.
My poems of many kinds.
I thank you, Lord, for my poems.

My Poems Are Like
My Prayers

My poems are like my prayers.
They tell my Lord Jesus Christ, Savior,
My heavenly Father, how I feel and what I think.
When I'm sad, when I'm happy.
My poems are like my prayers.
They tell of many things—
Some about things, some about my feelings
And my thoughts.
Things that relate to my Lord Jesus Christ, Savior,
My heavenly Father.
Objects that go a long with you.
His forgiveness and caring for me.
His love for us.
His living, his dying and rising, his coming again—
He did it all for me.
My poems are like my prayers.
They tell of many things, and they tell
About my Jesus.
They're what I feel in my heart.
My poems are like my prayers.

My Times Are in Your Hands, Oh, Lord

My times are in your hands, oh, Lord.
Before I was born, even after I was born.
When I was a little girl, and when I was a teenage girl.
My times are in your hands, oh, Lord.
When loved ones pass away, there tears and sorrow.
When I'm sad, feel all alone.
My times are in your hands, Oh, Lord.
When I'm happy and carefree, when I have fun times,
And laughter.
My times are in your hands, oh, Lord.
When I asked you into my life and live for you.
When I pray to you, sing about you.
Read my Bible, go to church,
Teach my Sunday school class, praise your holy name,
My times are in your hands, oh, Lord.
When I trust you and believe in you.
You take care of me always.
When you have your loving arms around me.
My times are in your hands, oh, Lord.
When I grow old.
From the beginning to the end of my life.
When it's time to meet my Lord in heaven and live
For all eternity with you, Lord,
My times are in your hands, oh. Lord.
But I trust in you, oh, Lord.
I say you are my Lord.
My times are in your hands, oh, Lord.

Never Too Weary

God is never too weary to answer my prayers.
It's doesn't matter how big.
It doesn't matter how small.
All my prayers are important to God.
God is never too weary to answer my prayers.
Sometimes it may be no because God
Knows what's best for me.
Sometimes it may be yes.
Sometimes we might have to wait.
Sometimes it's different than we
Thought it would be but for the better.
All my prayers are important to God.
God is never too weary to answer my prayers.

No Doubt about It

No doubt about it,
One of these days an angel will come
For me, to take me to the pearly gates of heaven
For all eternity.
No doubt about it, Jesus will meet me
At the pearly gates.
I'll kiss his nail-print feet.
No doubt about it, Jesus will say, "Welcome
Home, my child."
No doubt about it.
I'll tell Jesus, "Thank you for coming
To earth as a baby.
For dying on the old rugged cross
For my sins, for rising again to show
Me you love me."
I'll thank him for letting me live in heaven for all eternity.
No doubt about it, I'll walk the golden streets.
I'll have a mansion built for me.
No doubt about it, I'll be with my loved ones, family,
And friends in heaven.
I'll make new friends in heaven.
No doubt about it, I'll thank my guardian angel.
I'll live with all the angels in heaven.
I'll thank them for always taking care of me and protecting me.

No doubt about it, I'll get to talk with all the
Faithful people in the Bible.
I'll sing in the heavenly choir.

I'll walk by the Crystal Sea.
No doubt about it, I'll play with the children and the animals.
No doubt about it, I'll live for all eternity in heaven with God,
Jesus, and the Holy Ghost.
No doubt about it, God, Jesus, and The Holy Ghost
Will tell me they love me, and I'll tell them I love them too.
No doubt about it.

No Hesitation

No hesitation for all would be lost.
No hesitation for you can't make it on time to do
What the Lord wants.
When the Lord ask you to do,
Jump in and do as the Lord asks.
Tell others about the Lord,
When the Lord asks you to win others for him.
Don't hesitate for if you hesitate, all would be lost.
No hesitation would be best.
If you do hesitate and the time was lost,
Ask the Lord for forgiveness, and he will
Forgive and forget.
When the Lord asks you to win souls for him,
You would not want to hesitate again.
No hesitation is what you want for yourself,
For souls of people, and for the Lord.
For you will feel the joy yourself for winning souls for the Lord.
For all will rejoice in heaven.
Praise the Lord, no more hesitation.

No More Tears

No more tears when I reach the glory land.
Through the pearly gate I will walk to meet my Jesus.
No more tears in heaven, no more burdens to carry.
No more trouble when I reach the glory land.
No more tears, no more sorrow.
No more sins when I reach the glory land.
No more tears, only praises for my Lord.
Shouting glory,
Hallelujah.
No more tears when I get to heaven.
Praise Jesus's holy name.
No more tears.

Now I Have Everything

I was nothing to no one, but now I'm something to Jesus.
I'm his for all eternity.
He's the one who cares for me.
Now I have everything.
I have everything because he died for me.
I was alone, and no one cared for me.
But Jesus, he's always there for me.
Now I have everything.
When I'm lonely and feel like crying,
When I feel down, and that no one cares.
Jesus is there; he cares for me, he feels
what I feel, he knows what I'm going through.
Because he was there too.
He's always there for me.
Now I have everything.

Oftentimes Sorrow

Oftentimes he allows sorrow, so I can learn to lean on him.
"Trust in me," God says. "Don't rely on yourself but turn to me.
I'll help you through, no matter what the sorrow may be."
He tells me, "You have sorrow to make it to heaven.
It'll make you strong in me," God says. "Oftentimes
When you have sorrow, then you have the mountaintops
With me," says God.
"Trust in me," God says. "I'll see you through your sorrow.
I'll make you strong in me."
Oftentimes he allows me sorrow,
And praise God's holy name, he sees me through
And gives me his mountaintops.

On That Silent
Night Long Ago

It was a silent night long ago.
Shepherds watching their sheep.
Stars twinkling, sheep sleeping.
Lo, what do the shepherds hear?
Angels singing praises about the
newborn King.
A bright star overlooking Bethlehem,
Above a stable on that silent night a
Long time ago.
Mary and Joseph watching over baby
Jesus, sleeping in a manger.
Shepherds bowing down before him.
The donkey that carried Mary seems
To know that baby Jesus is the
King; that baby Jesus was the King
On that silent night long ago.
Three wise men follow a bright star,
Bringing gold, frankincense, and myrrh
To lay before baby Jesus on that
Silent night long ago.
On this Christmas Day, let us give
Ourselves to baby Jesus because
On that silent night long ago,
He came to give himself to us.
Merry Christmas, baby Jesus.

One Day at a Time

One day at a time, Jesus, that is only
What I'm asking for.
Help me to live for you,
Jesus, each day of my life.
Help me to be what you want me to be.
Help me to live each day according to your will.
Where I go, what I do, and what I say, let it be Jesus.
It'll be all for thee.
Whatever each day will bring, Jesus, help me
To live for thee.
Help me to live one day at a time.

One More Time

One more time, even though I've said it before,
I want to say it again.
Thank you for all you have done for me, and
Thank you for all the things you will still do for me.
When I'm sick, you make me well.
When I'm sad, you make me happy.
When I cry, you dry my tears.
You make me laugh.
You give me peace.
When I make a mess of my life, you straighten
Up my life.
When my burdens seem to be too much,
You see me through them.
You're always there for me.
One more time, even though I've said it before,
I want to say it again.
I love you more than words can say;
I love you more every day.
I want to say, "Thank you, God, for loving me.
Thank you for giving me Jesus.
Thank you, Holy Spirit, for living in my heart.
Thank you for saving me from my sins
And for dying on the cross for my sins.
For rising up; one of these days you'll come again."

I'll live for all eternity in heaven.
One more time, even though I've said it again,
I want to say it again.
I want to thank you for my guardian angel.
He can always take care of me and protect me

From the past and the future, when I knew it and
When I didn't know it.
One more time, even though I've said it
before, I want to say it again.
Thank you that I can live all eternity in heaven with my loved ones
And friends and angels.
Especially that I can live with you, my Lord
Jesus Christ, my heavenly Father, God,
And Holy Spirit.
I want to say thank you for everything.
One more time, even though I've said it before,
I want to say it again, thank you.

Open Heart, Open Arms

Open your arms Lord as I open my heart.
I say, "Yes, Lord," and you say, "I forgive and forget."
All my sins and shame, I give them all to you, Lord.
Lord, you say, "I take them all from you,
As I forgive and forget."
Lord, I open my heart; you open your arms.
Lord, I know now you forgive and forget.
For Lord, I'm in your arms of love.
My heart is open wide to you.
Your love, Lord, is all for me.
I open my heart; you open your arms.
Lord, I come into your arms as you
Forgive and forget: Open heart, open arms.

Our Home

Home so warm, home with so much love.
Home with so much caring and sharing.
Lord, thank you for my home and my family.
My love for them, them for me.
Home so cozy; home, a tender loving home.
The Lord is in our home.
The heavenly Father is in our home.
Home with lots of prayers.
Home with the Bible open to be read all the times.
Home sweet home, where our Lord is.
Our home.

Paradise

One of these days I'll go to paradise; it'll be my home
In heaven for all eternity.
I'll walk through the pearly gates.
I'll walk the golden streets.
I'll live in paradise.
I'll sing in the heavenly choir.
I'll thank my guardian angel for taking care of me.
I'll rejoice with all the angels in heaven.
I'll play with all the animals.
I'll live in paradise.
I'll love and play with all the children.
I'll be with my family, relatives, and friends.
I'll talk with the Bible people.
I'll live in paradise one of these days.
I'll praise Jesus's holy name; I'll kiss his nail-print feet
When I first get to heaven.
I'll praise God and thank him for giving his Son to die
On the cross for my sins so I can live in heaven
With him for all eternity.
I'll thank the Holy Spirit for living in my heart.
I'll thank my Savior and Lord, Jesus Christ
For dying on the cross for my sins.
I can live in heaven for all eternity.
Paradise.

Peace in the Storm of Life

I was out on a dark, cold, stormy night.
Out on the sea, the waves splashing
Onto my face.
The boat is about to turn over, and I
Think I'm going to drown.
I'm scared; I'm tired of battling the storm.
I'm tired of rowing to get to safety.
"Help," I call out. "Save me. Get me to safety. Keep me
Safe from the storm."
Then Jesus comes and says, "Peace be still in the
Storm is calm." It stops raining, and there's peace.
This is the way my life is.
The storm of life surrounds me.
Troubles, sorrows, grief, and pain; you feel
Like you're going to drown in it all.
It never seems to stop; it seems dark, and cold in my life.
I feel all alone; I'm scared, tired of fighting.
"Help," I call to Jesus. "I can't take all the storms in my life.
I give it all to you, Jesus."
Jesus comes to me and says, "Peace be still. I'm here for you,
I'm here for you. I'm always here for you.
I'm always here to give you peace, just like before.
Just believe, have faith, and trust me because I'll always
Calm the storms of life."
The storm of life will come, and it will go, and Jesus
Says, "I'll always be with you through all the storms of life."

The storms of life will come, and it will go, and Jesus
Says, "I'll always be with you through all the storms of life.
The storms of life will make you strong in me.

Remember, my child," said Jesus, "the storms of your life
Will be worth it all when you see me face-to-face and live
For all eternity in heaven with me.
Peace be still, my child, for you will always have peace
In heaven for all eternity."
Peace in the storm of life.

Pearl

Pearl of life, pearl of love.
Jesus, you gave me a pearl in my heart.
It shines of love for you.
You're a pearl to me, you're a pearl
Of love to me.
Pearl of love you gave to me.
Pearl of life, pearl of love.
Pearl that shines for others
From above; that's what you
Give to me, Jesus.
You're my pearl of life, pearl of love.
Pearl of kindness and caring.
Pearl of praying and sharing.
Pearl of many things you give
To me, Jesus.
Pearl of life, pearl of love.

Pearl of Life, Pearl of Love

Jesus, you gave me a pearl in my heart.
It shines of love for you.
You're a pearl to me; you're a pearl of life to me.
Pearl of love you gave me.
Pearl that shines for others from above,
That's what you give to me, Jesus.
You're my pearl of life, pearl of love.
Pearl of kindness and caring.
Pearl of praying and sharing.
Pearl of many things you give
to me, Jesus.
Pearl of life, pearl of life.
Pearl.

Picture for Thee

Pictures of many kind, many shapes, many sizes.
Jesus, help me to be a picture for thee.
Show my life like a picture; help them see you in me.
Picture with mountains, like my life when I'm up.
Picture with valleys, like my life when I'm down.
Picture with many shapes.
These pictures make me the way I should be.
Jesus, make me a picture for thee.

Praise His Name

Praise his name, his holy name.
He gives me joy within my heart.
The love he shows me, the peace
Within me he gives.
Praise his name, his holy name.
His wonderful grace, he died for me on a old rugged tree.
He rose from the grave to make me free from sin and shame.
Praise his name, his holy name.
There're no words to tell him how much
I love him for he first loved me.
Jesus, praise your name, your holy name.
Praise his name.

Praise Jesus's Holy Name

Praise his holy name, praise his name, let the whole world
Praise Jesus's holy name.
Give him glory, give him glory.
Let the whole world praise Jesus's holy name.
Show him love, show him love.
Sing his praises, sing his praises.
Let the whole world praise Jesus's holy name.
Kneel down before him, kneel down before him.
Give him thanks, give him thanks.
Let the whole world praise Jesus's holy name.
Praise Jesus's holy name.

Praises to His Name

Praises to his name, his only name.
He's fairer to me than anything.
Praises to his name, his holy name.
He is Lord to me; he's fairer than the lilies.
Brighter than the morning star.
His kindness is more than any words can tell.
Praise his name, his holy name, his holy name.
He's King of Kings to me.
He loves his children more than we can know.
We mean more to him than anything.
Praise his holy name, his holy name.
Praises to his name.

Praises to You, God

Praises to you God, praises to you.
Thank you for helping me, keeping me.
You're so good to me.
Praises to you, God, praises to you.
You're so wonderful to me.
You give me happiness in my soul.
You help me in everything.
Praises to you, God, praises to you.
You mean so much to me, more than words can ever tell.
All I can say is praises to you,
praises to you, God,
praises to you.

Prayers for Thee

Prayers for thee, my friends, family, and relatives.
Prayers for me.
I give them all, Lord, to thee.
Let me show forth my cares through prayers.
My prayers to the Lord and Savior.
That's how I talk with him, through my prayers.
Prayers of love and concerns.
Prayers of happiness, prayers of thankfulness,
Prayers of sadness; Lord, I give them all to thee.
Prayers for thee, my friends and family and relatives.
Prayers for me.
I give them all, Lord, to thee.
Prayers of many kinds, small, big, it doesn't matter
At all; I give them, Lord, all to thee.
Lord, you listen, you care.
You lift us up, you work them out the way
That's best for them and me.
Prayers, my friends, family, and relatives.
Prayers for me, I give them all, Lord, to thee.
Prayers for thee.

Put Your Arms
around Me Tight

Lord, put your arms around me; put them around me tight.
Cover me, protect me with your comforting arms
Against earth's sin and shame.
Keep me close to your arms of love.
Put your arms around me; put them around me tight.
I want to feel your arms of comfort.
Keep me close to you, away from anything wrong.
Put your arms around me; put them around me tight.
Thank you, Lord, for I do feel your arms of love around me.
Thank you, Lord, for putting your arms around me,
Putting them around me tight.

Put Your Trust in the Lord

Put your trust in the Lord.
When you're sad and you shed many tears,
Put your trust in the Lord.
When you don't know where to turn,
Remember to turn to the Lord.
When you don't know what life will bring,
Put your trust in the Lord.
When your burdens seem more than
You can bear,
Your sorrow seems to bear down on you,
Put your trust in the Lord.
The Lord tells you, "I'm here with you always."
The Lord tells you, "I'm here when you're sad,
And shed many tears."
The Lord tells you, "I'm here when you don't
Know what life will bring."
The Lord tells you, "I'm with you when your
Burdens seem more than you can bear."
The Lord tells you, "I'm with you when your
Sorrow seems to bear down on you."
The Lord tells you, "Put your trust in me.
I'll be with you always, no matter
What life will bring."
The Lord tells you, "I'll take care of you
Through everything in your life."
The Lord tells you, "Put your trust in me."
Put your trust in the Lord.

Rainbow in the Sky

As I look up in the sky, I see a rainbow so bright.
After every rain, God promises us a rainbow in the sky.
It doesn't matter if morning, noon, evening, or night.
After every rain, God gives us a rainbow in the sky.
There're so many colors in the rainbow—
Blue, pink, yellow, lavender, and green.
Rainbow in the sky, how bright you are with so many
Colors to see; 'tis so true God's promise to see
Rainbow in the sky after every rain.
Rainbow in the sky.

Rain That God Made

Rain falling down my face, wet and cold,
Or sometimes warm or cool.
Raindrops big or small, God made them all.
Rain puddles, rain splashing in the puddles.
God made the rain; he made it wet.
Rain in the spring, rain in the summer.
Rain that God made at different times.
How nice to splash in the puddles of rain.
When young, how nice it was to feel the water on my feet
And feel the drops of rain as it fell on my face.
Rain that God made.
Puddles at my feet.
Raindrops on my face.
Wet, so cool, warm, cold on my face.
Rain that God made.

It was always fun to feel the rain coming
Down my grandparents R.'s eaves trough
From there home, on to me.

Rejoice, Rejoice

Rejoice, rejoice, my people, how I live, I rose
After death on a cross.
I am Lord of all.
Rejoice, rejoice for I'm coming again for my loved ones.
Rejoice, rejoice for one Easter morn I rose for all your sins.
Rejoice, rejoice, I fought. and I won the battle; I have the key.
Rejoice, rejoice, I'm Jesus, your King for all eternity.
Rejoice, rejoice, I'll always love you.
Rejoice, rejoice.

Rescue 911

When you need help and you're in trouble,
Whom do you call?
Call rescue 911.
Jesus is our rescue 911.
When our hearts are in sin, when we do the wrong things,
Call rescue 911; Jesus is our rescue 911.
Jesus will answer you.
Jesus will forgive us of our sins.
Our hearts will have love and happiness and peace.
When we feel troubled, our burdens seem way
Too heavy on our hearts.
Whom do we call?
Rescue 911, and Jesus will answer your call.
Jesus will lift your burdens off your heart.
Make your heart happy again.
If we need help, whom do we call?
We call Jesus to help.
We read our Bibles and pray and go to church.
Jesus will always be with us.
Whom do we call for help?
We call rescue 911; Jesus is our rescue 911.

Ring! Ring!

Ring! Ring! Ring the bell.
Do you hear the bells on Sunday morning?
They're calling you to church and to serve the Lord.
Ring! Ring! Ring! Do you hear the bells loud and clear,
Saying come to church and hear about Jesus and
How much he loves us and cares for us?
Ring! Ring! Ring the bells and come to church and learn
About Jesus and how he loves us.
He cares for us, protect us, and makes us feel peace in our hearts.
He's near to us all the time.
Jesus wants us to serve him.
Ring! Ring! Ring the bells.

Room for One More

In heaven, where there are holy angels and saints,
There's room for one more.
Little boys and girls,
Ask Jesus into your hearts and live for him.
There's room for one more in heaven.
Teenage girls and boys, ask Jesus into your hearts.
In heaven there are holy angels and saints,
And there's room for one more.
Mothers, fathers, aunts, uncles,
Grandpas, grandmas, cousins,
Ask Jesus into your hearts.
There's room for one more.
Single, married people,
Friends and strangers, ask Jesus into your hearts.
There's room for one more.
Middle-aged, older people, young people,
Ask Jesus into your hearts.
There's room for one more.
The Lord Jesus Christ and my God, our heavenly Father,
Will be there to welcome you into heaven.
There's room for you too.
There's room for one more.

Roses, so Wonderful

Oh, how beautiful roses are.
It's so wonderful that God could make roses of many colors.
You can be as red as a ruby
But as yellow as the sun.
Can even make them as white as snow,
Even pink as the sunsets.
Your petals can be as soft as silk, but your thorns can
Be hard with stickers.
As I touch your petals against my face, they're soft as satin.
How I love to feel your petals so much against my face.
It's wonderful that God could make something like you.
Roses of many colors, roses of soft petals, some with many thorns.
You're wonderful to me.
Roses, so wonderful.

Secret Pal Revealing Time

So it's revealing time again for secret pal!
Who could my secret pal be?
Is it you or you or even you?
Because I know it's not me!
We give with love and prayers; we give
With happiness and joy.
The joy of giving gifts secretly to see the
Faces of joy when they don't know you're looking,
When they see what they have.
You will pray for your secret pal, that Jesus
Will keep his hand on her.
Then the joy and excitement of getting a gift,
Looking around, wondering who your secret pal
Could be, know your secret pal will pray for you.
So it's revealing time again for a secret pal!
Who could my secret pal be?
Is it you or you, or even you?
Because I know it's not me!
Oh, what a surprise; it was you!
I couldn't have guessed even once.
Thank you, secret pal, for your gifts of love
And praying for me.
I was your secret pal; I know you didn't know.
What a surprise for you that it was me,
Who gave from love and prayers for you.
Secret pal revealing time.

Since Jesus Came In

Since Jesus came into my heart,
oh, Jesus, give me great joy.
The joy in my heart I'll always have.
A song I'll always have with a smile
In my heart.
Jesus put a smile on my face
Since I let him in.
Since Jesus came into my heart,
He gives me joy and happiness.
Since Jesus came into my heart,
oh, the peace that's come into my heart;
It is there to stay.
Oh, the love and the caring that are
There to stay
Since Jesus came into my heart.

Sleep, My Child

Sleep, my child.
Sleep quickly, sleep restfully, keep your trust in me.
Sleep all night; I'll keep you from all harm.
Sleep my child; I'm watching you, keeping you safe.
Sleep my child; dream of happiness, peace.
I'm there at all times.
Sleep my child. I'll keep you safe. I'll watch over you.
Rest all night, my child; Jesus is watching you all night long.
"Sleep, my child," Jesus tells us.
Sleep my child.

Snowflakes

Snowflakes fall softly down.
So white, so fluffy how it comes down
Wet on my face.
Oh, cold you are.
My heavenly Father, I thank you for the many
Kinds of snowflakes.
It doesn't matter how many come down, each one
Is different from the other.
Some are small, some are big, each one made
In its own way and size.
Heaven Father, I thank you for each different snowflake.
Some snowflakes are so big and fluffy, they're like chicken feathers
Falling from the sky.
Oh, there are so many shapes and sizes.
It's something that God can give us so many different snowflakes.
Oh, snowflakes that fall so softly down, you're really something
Because God made you.
Snowflakes.

Someone Who Cares

There's someone who cares for you.
If there's someone who cares for me,
Why am I like I am,
The kind of person I am?
There's someone who cares for you like no one ever would.
If you had been the only person in this world,
He still would have died for you.
Who is this someone who cares for me?
I would like to meet him.
The one who cares for you is Jesus.
He came as a babe in a manger,
Grew to be a man to tell others about how their souls
Could be saved.
Then died on an old rugged cross and then rose
again after three days.
He lives forever in heaven; he will come again someday
For the ones who live for him to take them to heaven
For eternity.
Would you like for him to come into your heart today?
Because he's the one who cares for you.
Yes, I would like for him to come in to stay.
Thank you for sharing with me for now I know
There's someone who cares for me.
I'm glad I shared with you for now you know that
There is someone who cares for you.

Sorrow into Joy

Sorrow into joy, that's what I will take
When the sorrow I must have to strengthen me
And draw me closer, Lord, to you.
Then joy it will be after the sorrow.
My joy will be complete; What joy, Lord!
With you I'll have sorrow into joy.
Oh, the sorrow I sometimes have, but
Then, oh, what joy I'll have in my heart
With the Lord.
Lord, I'll have sorrow into joy.

Star of Jesus Christ

Star that shines down on us,
Keep us, watch us.
Shine on us, star of Jesus Christ.
When things seem dark and lost,
Shine on us, star of Jesus Christ.
When life seems so much we can't go on,
Shine down on us, star of Jesus Christ.
Star of Jesus Christ, give us faith, hope, and love.
Star of Jesus Christ, carry us through our changing lives.
Star of Jesus Christ, shine on us with brightness of life.
Star of Jesus Christ.

Statue of Liberty

Statue of Liberty, lady tall, lighted torch,
Show forth your light.
Bring in the lost, bring in the lonely, crying.
Statue of Liberty, lady of light, shine bright.
Lord of all, give me a light, a torch for the lost.
Help me to bring in the lonely, the crying,
The lost, so they will live for the Lord.
Statue of Liberty, lady tall, shine your torch
For the lost; bring them in one by one, two by two.
Bring them in more and more, one and all,
And I'll shine my torch for the Lord of all.
And shine my torch for the Lord of all.
Shine forth, Statue of liberty.
Statue of Liberty.

Take My Life, Jesus

Take my life, Jesus; let it be all for thee—
Whatever it may be.
All for thee, my life shall be.
Take my life, Jesus, make it out what thee
Shall please.
For thee shall know what's best for me.
Take my life, Jesus, make it out in thy
Own special way.
Take my life, Jesus; make it better for me.
I will seek thee, Jesus, and know thee.
Help me to be more like thee.
Take my life, Jesus, make it
More like thee.

Teardrops

I can feel the teardrops falling down my face
Whenever I think of how much you love me, Jesus.
You must love me so much to come to earth
As a baby, just like me.
You grew up into a child, just like me.
I can feel the teardrops falling down my face.
You had a mother and father to love you
And to show you the way to live, teach you about God
And his love for you; you love God.
Just like I did.
I feel your love for me.
You grew up, just like I did.
I know you went through the same things I did and do.
You know how it is to live here on earth, like I do.
I feel the teardrops falling down my face.
I know you love me for you went through the same things I do.
You had the burdens, sadness, pain, sorrow, grief, and
Tears, just like I do.
I know you love me for you went through
the same things I did and do.
You had good times, happy times, fun,
laughter, and joy, like I did and do.
I feel the teardrops falling down my face.
I can feel the love you have for me, and I do know you love me.

You preached, teacher.
There were people who respected you, loved
you, and wanted to be with you,
Just like I do.
There were people who made fun of you, ridiculed you.

This makes me sad that there were people like that.
I feel the teardrops falling down my face.
The people tortured you, hung you on the old rugged cross,
With nails in your hands and feet, and a spear thrust in your side.
The pain you must have suffered; you must have felt all alone.
It's more than I can comprehend, but I know
you love me to go through all this.
I feel the teardrops falling down my face.
I feel your love for me.
Then you arose and came back, and then went to heaven
To show everyone you love us, you forgive us our sins.
One of these days you'll come back to take us to heaven
For all eternity.
One of these days I'll live with you in heaven for eternity.
I love you, Jesus, because you first loved me.
I feel the teardrops falling down my face.

Tie One More Knot

Tie one more knot.
When things seem bad, tie a knot
In the rope and hang on.
When things seem to go from bad to worse,
Just tie one more knot in the rope
And hang on.
The knot seems to come undone in the rope, and
You seem to slip and fall.
Just tie one more knot in the rope
And hang on.
When you don't know what else to do,
Where else to go,
Just tie one more knot in the rope
And hang on.
You don't want to give up, or you want to go on,
But you don't know how you can.
Just tie one more knot in the rope
And hang on.
When your life seems to fall apart,
When your life seems too hard to face,
Just tie one more knot in the rope and hang on.
When you're sad and you're crying because of things in your life,
When you're in pain or sick, what can you do? You ask Jesus.
Just tie one more knot in the rope and hang on.
You wonder why you have to go through all the bad things
In your life; you ask, "Why, Jesus, does this have to be?"
Just tie one more knot in the rope and hang on.
All the things you go through will make your faith strong in Jesus
And help to lean on him and live for him.

Just tie one more knot in the rope and hang on.
For one of these days it'll be worth it all
Because you'll live in heaven with Jesus for eternity.
Just tie one more knot in the rope and hang on.
Tie one more knot.

The Angel Gave Good News

The angel came to tell us some good news.
There's a little baby born this Christmas morn.
He's Jesus Christ, our Savior, he's here to save us
from our sins.
See all the angels there to give him their gift of songs
Of praise this Christmas Day.
The angels came to tell us some good news.
See the bright star up in the sky overlooking
The town of Bethlehem?
The shepherds saw and heard the angels
Telling of the coming of baby Jesus.
So the shepherds came to bow down to worship him.
The three wise men followed the star to Bethlehem to a manger.
They came and gave baby Jesus frankincense, gold, and myrrh.
The angels came to tell us some good news.
There, do you see under the bright star a stable with baby Jesus
Asleep in a manger with Mary and Joseph watching over him?
The cows and sheep sleep peacefully by.
The donkey that carried Mary to Bethlehem seems to know
How special baby Jesus is. The angels
came to tell us some good news.
So let us sing our praises along with the angels to baby Jesus
This Christmas Day.
So this Christmas Day,
Let us give ourselves to Jesus because Jesus is God's gift to us.
Merry Christmas, Jesus.

The Cross

To the garden he had gone to pray.
The anguish he must have felt.
As he prayed there were sweat-like drops of blood.
As he prayed, "My Father, do I have to go through this?"
But thy will be done.
Then the soldiers came to take him away.
They spat on him, mocked him.
They gave him a crown of thorns and put a
Purple robe on him.
Pontias asked, "Who should we release, Bartimaeus
or Jesus?"
The people said to crucify Jesus, he was to blame.
He carried the cross to Golgotha hill.
The two crosses, one on each side.
They did the crimes for which they were accused.
But the middle cross, where Jesus was, what did he do?
He was innocent, but they put him there anyway.
The sign said, "He's the king of the Jews."
Why was the one in the middle, the one called Jesus,
Why did they put him there?
He was innocent; why did Jesus let them put him there
When he could have called ten thousand angels to set him free?

His hands and feet were nailed to the middle cross.
Why did he love us so much to die on the cross for us?
The middle cross, where he was nailed on,
Ridiculed, mocked, laughed at.
It should have been us on that middle cross to endure
All the sins we have done.
But the one on the middle cross—Jesus—took our place.

He took the guilt, shame, all our sins on himself.
He did it all for us, to set us free.
Praise Jesus's holy name for being nailed to the middle cross.
The cross was where my Jesus was nailed and died.
Praise Jesus's holy name, after three days he arose.
One of these days he will come again for me.
The cross.

There's a Song in My Heart

There's a song in my heart, and song of praise,
A song of praise and joy you give me.
There's a song in my heart that Jesus gave me.
It'll stay there from year to year.
There's a song in my heart; it'll be there
For all eternity.
Jesus, you give me a song of peace, joy, and love.
There's a song in my heart.
A song for all times, a song that will be there
For ages to come, ages for all eternity.
There's a song in my heart.

That Day

Thank you, Lord for coming into my heart that day.
It didn't matter what I did, you forgave me all my sins that day.
You knocked at my heart's door; I'm glad
I let you come in that day.
You knocked at my heart's door; I'm glad
I let you come in that day.
I can't express what I feel or think.
The tears of joy or the laughter of your Spirit as I try to express
How I feel ever since that day you came into my heart.
I don't know what to say about how I feel; I want to cry with joy
And laugh in happiness for all you do for me
Ever since you knocked on my heart's door,
And I let you in that day.

The Lord Made Me

The Lord made me what he wanted me to be.
No one can change me, no matter how they try.
For I'm the way the Lord wanted me to be.
I'm just right for him.
No one can change me; no one can make me anew.
If he wants to change me, mold me, or make me
different and anew, he's the only one who can.
The Lord made me the way he wants me to be.
I'm his own special creation.
I'm one of a kind.
I'm his to be what he wants me to be.
I'm his and he's mine.
The Lord made me the way he wanted me to be.

The Middle Cross

Three crosses on Golgotha hill.
But only one I really see.
It's not the one on the cross who hurled insults at Jesus.
It's not the one on the cross who asked to be remembered
When Jesus went to heaven.
But it's the middle cross, where my Jesus was crucified.
They nailed his feet and hands to the middle cross.
His side was pierced. He wore a torn crown on his head.
How he must of suffered, but still he said, "Forgive them,
They do not know what they do"; and he forgives us too.
Each drop of blood he shed, he shed for us.
That's how much he loves each of us.
Jesus died on the old rugged cross for our sins.
Three crosses but only one I really see; it's the middle cross,
Where my Jesus hanged so we can be saved.
But he's not on the middle cross anymore.
Then they placed him in a grave, he was there for three days.
The angel said, "He's not here; he is risen."
He's alive, hallelujah, Jesus is alive.
God loves us so much that he gave us his Son, Jesus.
The middle cross where Jesus had hung, and then he arose
so we all can be saved, and he can live in our hearts and lives.
Praise Jesus's holy name; he will come again for his loved ones
so we can live in heaven for all eternity with him.
The middle cross.

The Nail Prints

The nail prints on your hands, dear Jesus,
They showed me you died for me.
The blood you shed for me.
The love you have for me.
The nails prints on your hands, dear Jesus,
They showed me you rose again for me.
You saved me from my sins.
You'll come back for me someday, dear Jesus.
I'll see the pearly gates and walk the street made of gold.
I'll live in heaven for eternity.
I'll see loved ones; I'll see friends.
I'll be with you, Jesus, for eternity.
The nails print on your hands, dear Jesus,
You did it all for me.
The nail prints.

The Potter, the Clay

Lord, you're the potter; I'm the clay, mold me.
Make me in thy own way; make me a vase
In the right way.
When I'm rough one way, make me smooth.
When I'm leaning another way,
Lord, as the potter, straighten me back up.
Lord, you're the potter, I'm the clay.
When I'm down, build me back up.
You the potter, I'm the clay; when I get some
Holes in me, patch them up and make me a vase
In thy own way.
Lord, you're the potter. I'm the clay, mold me,
Make me in thy own way.
Fill me, mold me, make me a new vase.
You're the potter, I'm the clay; make me a vase
In thy own way.
The potter, the clay.

Thank You, Heavenly Father

Thank you, heavenly Father, for my family.
Thank you for my home, so warm and loving.
Thank you for my praying mother and caring father.
Thank you for my loving sister.
Thank you for my two sweet nephews.
Thank you so much for all my pets I had, now have,
And will have for I love them, and I know they love me.
Thank you, heavenly Father for my loving family.
Thank you on this Thanksgiving Day and all
Thanksgiving days that I have with my family.
Thank you, heavenly Father for living with us
In our home and lives.
Thank you, heavenly Father for my loving family.
Thank you, heavenly Father for loving me.
I love you, heavenly Father.
Thank you, heavenly Father.

Thank You, Lord

Thank you, Lord, for all you've done for me.
For all the things you'll still do for me.
Even though I'm not worthy for all I was,
It didn't matter.
You cared enough to take away
All my sins and shame.
Thank you, Lord, for all you've done,
And for all you'll do for me.
For your love and all your care.
You're there all the time—when I'm down,
When I'm up.
You're the one for me; you're my life,
My all, my Savior divine.
Thank you, Lord, for all you've done
For me, for all things you'll do for me.
It doesn't matter how many times
I'll tell you thank you.
You're my all and all to me.
Thank you, Lord.

The Lord woke me up from a dream with this poem.

This Is Your Church, Lord

This is your church, Lord, so let the music play.
The voices sing, and people praise you.
The preacher preaches of your love, Lord.
Sunday school teachers teach the children.
We want to do this for you, Lord, in the house,
Your church.
Let us, Lord, pray to you on our knees.
We bow before you.
The reverence we have for you in our hearts.
The church, Lord, is a place of praise and worship.
We want this, Lord, in your church.
You're the leader, we're the followers.
We serve you in your house, the church, Lord.
This is your church, Lord.

Three Crosses

Three crosses on Golgotha hill.
But only one I really see.
It's not the one on the cross who asked
For forgiveness from my Lord.
It's not the one who condemned my Lord.
But it's the middle cross; the one they
Crucified was my Lord.
The nails in his hands and feet, and
His pierced sides,
The thorn crown on his head.
How he must have suffered, but he still
Said, "Forgive them they do not know what they do."
Each drop of blood he shed,
That's how much he loves us.
Jesus died on the old rugged cross for our sins.
Praise the Lord, praise his holy name.
He arose from the grave and ascended into heaven.
Praise the Lord, praise his holy name.
Praise his holy name; he will come again for his loved ones
To live in heaven for all eternity.
We'll praise Jesus's holy name.
Three crosses, but only one I really see; it's the middle cross.
That's my Jesus on the middle cross.
He shed his blood for me
To show me he loves me.
Three crosses.

Treasures and Saints

We are Jesus's little treasures; you are God's saints.
We have little hands; you have bigger hands.
Jesus can hold our little hands and make us safe.
God can hold your bigger hand and make you safe.
We have little hearts but lots of love.
You have big hearts and lots of love too.
Jesus loves little ones, and he loves bigger ones too.
We love Jesus, and so do you.
We're little and have lots more to learn about Jesus.
You're bigger and know more than we do about Jesus.
You are God's saints; you know more about Jesus.
When we grow up, we want to be his saints too.
We all are special in Jesus's and God's sight.
We are Jesus's little treasures.
You are God's saints.

From Jesus's Little Treasures Toddlers' class, two- and three-year-olds, which I taught and who taught it to the older people's class, the Lighthouse class.

To My Heavenly Home

Heaven-ward bound I must go to meet my Jesus.
So sweet and with his love so complete.
I'll meet him with his arms out wide, with him
Saying, "Welcome home, my child."
He will put his arms of love around me,
And I'll put my arms around him.
I'll say, "Thank you for everything." Then I'll say I'm happy
To be home with my Jesus to live
In heaven of rest.
My Jesus and I will be together to live in
Heaven for eternity.

Trees and leaves

I love to see the tree limbs blowing in the wind.
To see the green leaves blooming in the spring.
Or in the fall, when the leaves are falling on the ground,
Their green, yellow, red, and brown leaves beneath the trees.
And in the winter as the leaves lie beneath the snow.
How beautiful are the leaves in all the four seasons!
Trees can live to be hundreds of years old.
The trees and leaves are God's own creations
To show his love for us.
Trees and leaves.

What Is an American, People?

What is an American, people? It's everyone.
Not just one color, one kind, one race.
God made each person—each of us—to be an American.
All our ancestors came from all over the world.
What is an American? It's everyone.
You're red, yellow, black, and white.
You came from many countries.
What is an American, people? It's everyone.
God made you all; you come from a long time ago.
Each one came over to America, and as you came, we became
As one people.
God made the Native Americans; you were here
Before any of us; all of you are what is an American.
We the people are one; we are what are American people,
Each of us.
God made us all, and he loves all of us.
American people.

Who's That Man?

Who's that man who lived on earth for thirty-three years?
For three years he taught his disciples.
Who's that man who changed the water into wine,
Made the blind see?
Who's that man
Who calmed the storm?
He healed the leopard.
He raised the dead to life.
Who's that man
Who feed five thousand,
Who healed women, men, and children?
Who forgave men and women of their sins?
Who's that man
Who loves all little children,
Who listens to everyone,
Who loves everyone?
Who's that man
Who rode a donkey into Jerusalem
And wept over Jerusalem,
Who washed his disciples' feet,
Who broke bread for his broken body,
Who shared the wine for his shed blood?
Who prayed in the garden and shed drops of blood.
Who's that man
Who was beaten, spat on, mocked, and strapped,
Who carried his cross?
Who's that man?

Who forgave a man on the other cross, who died
On the cross, forgave all people of their sins?
Who's that man
Who rose from the grave,
Walked the earth for forty days?
Who's that man?
Who went to heaven and will come back again
To bring his loved ones to heaven one of these days?
Who's that man
Who came as a baby in a manger, then a
teenager, and became a man?
Who's that man?
Who knew how it is to live on earth and feel like other people?
Who's that man?

He's my Lord Jesus Christ; he's my Savior.
He forgave me all my sins.
I love him, and he loves me.
Who's that man?
He's my Jesus.

Who's That Riding on a Donkey

Who's that riding on a donkey,
With people waving palm branches,
robes played on the ground?
It's my Jesus, Lord of Lords.
Who's that riding on a donkey?
People singing and praising Jesus,
Singing "Hosanna" to the King of Kings.
The joy they must have felt!
It's my Jesus.
Who's that man on a donkey,
With tears in his eyes and running down his face,
With love in his heart?
It's my Jesus.
Who's that riding on a donkey
On that long-ago Palm Sunday through Jerusalem,
Getting ready to die on the old rugged cross for me,
And rise again to live for me and come again for me?
It's my Jesus; he did it all for me.
Who's that riding on a donkey?
It's my Jesus, riding on a donkey.

Windmill

The windmill goes around and around.
The life of toil goes around and around.
As the wind blows, the windmill goes
Around and around; so does God that lives in us
Moves us around and around, makes us to
Be the way that's best for us.
As the water runs, smooth and blue, or sometimes
Rough, it's up to the windmill.
So is our life like the water and the wind.
God makes us, molds us.
Sometimes life is rough, sometimes smooth.
God is always there to see us through.
Windmill goes around and around.
The wind blows, water runs with the windmill.
God goes with us whatever life may be.
Let us be windmills and run our lives
As God knows what's best for us.
Windmill.

Wonderful Mother

Wonderful Mother, you give me a song in my heart
And joy in my soul.
You give me happiness.
Mother, I'm glad God gave me to you and you to me.
You cared enough to love me, pray for me, worry about me,
Do little or big things for me.
You're a wonderful mother.
Mother, you're everything to me.
I love you more than words can tell or show.
Thank you, Mother, for loving me more than words
Can tell or show me.
Mother, I give you a mother's day every day
Because you're special to me.
Mother, you cry with me, laugh with me.
Mother, I'm glad you showed me the way of salvation,
Told me about Jesus.
I'm glad God gave you this gift of being the best
Mother in the world.
You're a wonderful mother to me.
Wonderful mother.

Ye of Little Faith

"Ye of little faith, trust in me; I'll see you through
Each and every thing, little or big.
Ye of little faith, trust in me; I'll keep you safe
From harm.
Ye of little faith, trust in me," says the Lord.
"I'm here to help you through bad times,
Good times; I'm here for you all times.
Ye of little faith, trust in me," says the Lord.
"Yes, Lord, thank you for helping me have faith.
I'll trust in you through all times.
I'll not be me in little faith.
I'll trust in you.
With your help. Lord, this will be."
Have more faith, not ye of little faith.

Yes, I Know

Yes, I know Jesus takes care of me.
Yes, I know Jesus took away my sins and lives in my heart.
Yes, I know Jesus takes away my sorrow and sadness
And gives me peace and happiness.
Yes, I know Jesus takes away my tears
And gives me laughter.
Yes, I know Jesus takes away my pain and sickness.
Yes, I know Jesus gives me my own guardian angel
To protect me.
Yes, I know God gave us his one and only begotten Son
so I can be saved from my sins.
Yes, I know I'll live for eternity in heaven with Jesus.
Yes, I know that Jesus loves me for the Bible tells me so.
Yes, I know.

You Don't Understand, but the Lord Does!

You don't understand, but the Lord does.
You feel sad all the time; all you want to do is cry.
Your tears fall down your face; they don't
Seem to stop falling.
You don't understand, but the Lord does.
The Lord will help you through everything.
You're confused, your heart aches.
The trouble you're going through doesn't
Seem to end.
You don't understand, but the Lord does.
You wonder why, so you ask the Lord, "Why?"
You pray that you don't understand,
But you tell him that you know he does.
You pray, "Help me, Lord, help me though
What I'm going through.
Help me, Lord, to understand; help me
To trust and believe you will help me
Through this."
The Lord tells you, "I'm here for you.
I'm holding you in my arms. I'll keep you safe.
I love you."
Then you feel the Lord's arms around you.
You feel comfort, and you feel at peace.
You pray, "I'm going to put my faith in you
To see me through all this.
I love you, Lord."
You don't understand, but the Lord does.

You're the Author of My Life

Lord, you're the Author of my life.
I'm your empty book; you write my
Life on the pages of my book—you're my Author.
Write my life from beginning to end.
Tell of my ups and downs, and how you always
See me through them.
You make me strong, Lord, in these times.
Lord, you're the Author of my life.
Write my life down in my book of the many
Things I've done for you.
You're my Author; I want, Lord, to live for you
The way you want me to.
Use me as a book to show others the way
To heaven.
As you the Author to write my life for you.
Author of my life; write my life in my book.
The ending will be I'll live in heaven for eternity.
Lord, you're the Author of my life.

Glossary

A

A Father Who Cares a Lot
An Old Year Has Gone, and a New Year Has Come
All Alone
All Alone But Jesus
As You See Me, Lord

B

Baby Boy
Baby Girl
Baby Jesus
Because My Name Is Written Down
Bell That Rings
Bible
Bubbly, Bubbly

C

Candle of Light
Candle So Bright
Children So Free
Christian Flag
Christmas Gift
Citizenship of Heaven
Come Follow Me
Come With Me, Jesus
Coming of Jesus

D

Don't Close the Little Country Church Doors
Don't Doubt

E

Ears to Hear
Easter in My Soul
Easter in My Soul
Easter Morn

F

Flag of America
For Me
For You
For All He Did
Friendship

G

Give Him Glory
Glory, Glory, Hallelujah
God Made Them All
God Made Many Things
God Made You Special, Lillian
Good Morning, Lord

H

Heavenly Things
Hear Ye! Hear Ye!
Help Me Be a Plant
How Do I Know He's the Lord?

Hummingbird
Hummingbird
Hurry! Hurry!

I

I Can't Comprehend
I Don't Know Why
I Feel Your Hand in My Hand, Jesus
I Just What You to Know
I Knew My Name Was Called
I Know My God Is With Me
I Love You, God
I Miss You, Mom
I Want You To
I Was There All the Time
If You Had Not
I'll Be Home Real Soon
I'll Be There Too
I'll Meet My Jesus
I'll Never Let Go, Jesus
I'm a Little Bit Closer Today Than Yesterday
I'm a Little Donkey
I'm a Little Drummer Boy
I'm Going to Heaven, and You Can't Stop Me
I'm Home at Last
I'm Home at Last
I'm Living for Him
I'm Not Poor
Impression on Me
In a Twinkling of an Eye

J

Jesus Is Just on Time
Jesus Is My Engineer
Jesus Is Our Gift to Us
Jesus Knocking
Jesus, My Pilot
Jesus, Please Help Me
Jesus, Take My Hand
Jesus Will See You Through
Jesus You're Many Flowers
Just a Whisper Away
Just Imagine

K

Key to Happiness
Key to Heaven
Kite of Life

L

Lead Me, God
Let Go, Let Me Work
Liberty and Justice
Life Is Stairsteps to Heaven
Lighthouse
Like an Eagle
Little Angel on Christmas Day
Little Bell
Little Bird
Little Bit of Love
Little Drops of Dew
Lord, Be the Anchor of My Soul

Lord, Thank You
Lord, Let Me See

M

Mend a Broken Heart
Mend My Broken Heart
Mirror of Reflection
More Than Just a Mother
Mother
Mother Like Mine
Mother Like Mine
Mustard Seed
My Father
My God Is Bigger
My Guardian Angel
My Little Feet
My Little Hands
My Mother
My Mother's Eyes
My Mother Is a Rose
My Mother Told Me about Jesus
My Poems Are Like My Prayers
My Times Are in Your Hands, Oh Lord

N

Never to Weary
No Doubt about It
No Hesitation
No More Tears
Now I Have Everything

O

Oftentimes Sorrow
On That Silent Night Long Ago
One Day at a Time
One More Time
Open Heart, Open Arms
Our Home

P

Paradise
Peace in the Storm of Life
Pearl
Pearl of Life, Pearl of Love
People of the Ghettos of New York
Picture for Thee
Praise His Name
Praise Jesus, Holy Name
Praise to His Name
Praises to You, God
Prayers for Thee
Put Your Arms Around Me Tight
Put Your Trust in the Lord

R

Rainbow in the Sky
Rain That God Made
Rejoice, Rejoice
Rescue 911
Ring, Ring
Room for One More
Roses So Wonderful

S

Secret Pal Revealing Time
Since Jesus Came In
Sleep, My Child
Someone Who Cares
Sorrow into Joy
Star of Jesus Christ
Statue of Liberty

T

Take My Life Jesus
Tear Drops
Tie One More Knot
Thank You, My Guardian Angel
The Angel Gave Good News
The Cross
There's a Song in My Heart
That Day
The Lord Made Me
The Middle Cross
The Nail Prints
The Potter, the Clay
Thank You, Heavenly Father
Thank You, Lord
This Is Your Church, Lord
Three Cross
Treasures and Saints
To My Heavenly Home
Trees and Leaves

W

What Is an American People?
Who's That Man?
Who's That Riding on a Donkey?
Windmill
Wonderful Mother
Worth It All

Y

Ye of Little Faith
Yes, I Know
You Don't Understand, but the Lord Does
You're the Author of My Life

Printed in the United States
By Bookmasters